[redacted]

LOVE, STRI
& CHANGI

LOVE, STRUGGLE & CHANGE

STORIES BY WOMEN

EDITED BY IRENE ZAHAVA

THE CROSSING PRESS
Freedom, California 95019

Grateful acknowledgment is made for permission to use the following previously published material:

"Giving Birth," from *Dancing Girls and Other Stories*, by Margaret Atwood. Copyright © 1977, 1982 by O.W. Toad, Ltd. Reprinted by permission of Simon and Schuster, Inc.

"Christmas Eve At Johnson's Drugs N Goods," from *The Sea Birds Are Still Alive*, by Toni Cade Bambara. Copyright © 1974, 1976, 1977 by Toni Cade Bambara. Reprinted by permission of Random House, Inc.

"In The Deep Heart's Core," from *Lovers' Choice*, by Becky Birtha. Copyright © 1987 by Becky Birtha. Reprinted by permission of The Seal Press.

"One Summer," excerpted from *Three Summers: A Journal*, by Yvonne Pepin. Copyright © 1986 by Yvonne Pepin. Reprinted by permission of Shameless Hussy Press.

The lyrics to "Don't Explain" are by B. Holiday and A. Herzog, Jr. Northern Music Co. (ASCAP).

The lines from *Where the Wild Things Are* are by Maurice Sendak.

Cover art and design by Diana Souza
Book design and production by Martha Waters
text in Goudy Old Style 12/13.5, titles in Artcraft

Printed in the U.S.A.

Library of Congress Cataloging-in-Publication Data

Love, struggle & change: stories by women/edited by Irene Zahava.

1. Short stories, American--Women authors. 2. Women--Fiction.
I. Zahava, Irene. II. Title: Love, struggle, and change.
PS647.W6L68 1988 813'.01'089287--dc19
ISBN 0-89594-264-X 87-34916
ISBN 0-89594-263-1 (pbk.) CIP

Contents

Giving Birth

Margaret Atwood

But who gives it? And to whom is it given? Certainly it doesn't feel like giving, which implies a flow, a gentle handing over, no coercion. But there is scant gentleness here, it's too strenuous, the belly like a knotted fist, squeezing, the heavy trudge of the heart, every muscle in the body tight and moving, as in a slow-motion shot of a high-jump, the faceless body sailing up, turning, hanging for a moment in the air, and then—back to real time again—the plunge, the rush down, the result. Maybe the phrase was made by someone viewing the result only: in this case, the rows of babies to whom birth has occurred, lying like neat packages in their expertly wrapped blankets, pink or blue, with their labels Scotch Taped to their clear plastic cots, behind the plate-glass window.

No one ever says *giving death*, although they are in some ways the same, events, not things. And *delivering*, that act the doctor is generally believed to perform: who delivers what? Is it the mother who is delivered, like a prisoner being released? Surely not; nor is the child delivered to the mother like a letter through a slot. How can you be both the sender and the receiver at once? Was someone in bondage, is someone made free? Thus language, muttering in its archaic tongues of something, yet one more thing, that needs to be re-named.

It won't be by me, though. These are the only words I have, I'm stuck with them, stuck in them. (That image of the tar sands, old tableau in the Royal Ontario Museum, second floor north, how persistent it is. Will I break free, or will I be sucked down, fossilized, a sabre-toothed tiger or lumbering brontosaurus who ventured out too far? Words ripple at my feet, black, sluggish, lethal. Let me try once more, before the sun gets me, before I starve or drown, while I can. It's only a tableau after all, it's only a metaphor. See, I can speak, I am not trapped, and you on your part can understand. So we will go ahead as if there were no problem about language.)

This story about giving birth is not about me. In order to convince you of that I should tell you what I did this morning, before I sat down at this desk—a door on top of two filing cabinets, radio to the left, calendar to the right, these devices by which I place myself in time. I got up at twenty-to-seven, and, halfway down the stairs, met my daughter, who was ascending, autonomously she thought, actually in the arms of her father. We greeted each other with hugs and smiles; we then played with the alarm clock and the hot water bottle, a ritual we go through only on the days her father has to leave the house early to drive into the city. This ritual exists to give me the illusion that I am sleeping in. When she finally decided it was time for me to get up, she began pulling my hair. I got dressed while she explored the bathroom scales and the mysterious white altar of the toilet. I took her downstairs and we had the usual struggle over her clothes. Already she is wearing miniature jeans, miniature T-shirts. After this she fed herself: orange, banana, muffin, porridge.

We then went out to the sun porch, where we recognized anew, and by their names, the dog, the cats and the birds, blue jays and goldfinches at this time of year, which is winter. She puts her fingers on my lips as I pronounce these words; she hasn't yet learned the secret of making them. I am waiting for her first word: surely it will be miraculous, something that has never yet been said. But if so, perhaps she's already said it and I, in my entrapment, my addiction to the usual, have not heard it.

In her playpen I discovered the first alarming thing of the day. It was a small naked woman, made of that soft plastic from which jiggly spiders and lizards and the other things people hang in their car windows are also made. She was given to my daughter by a friend, a woman who does props for movies, she was supposed to have been a prop but she wasn't used. The baby loved her and would crawl around the floor holding her in her mouth like a dog carrying a bone, with the head sticking out one side and the feet out the other. She seemed chewy and harmless, but the other day I noticed that the baby had managed to make a tear in the body with her new teeth. I put the woman into the cardboard box I use for toy storage.

But this morning she was back in the playpen and the feet were gone. The baby must have eaten them, and I worried about whether or not the plastic would dissolve in her stomach, whether it was toxic. Sooner or later, in the contents of her diaper, which I examine with the usual amount of maternal brooding, I knew I would find two small pink plastic feet. I removed the doll and later, while she was still singing to the dog outside the window, dropped it into the garbage. I am not up to finding tiny female arms, breasts, a head, in my daughter's disposable diapers, partially covered by undigested carrots and the husks of raisins, like the relics of some gruesome and demented murder.

Now she's having her nap and I am writing this story. From what I have said, you can see that my life (despite these occasional surprises, reminders of another world) is calm and orderly, suffused with that warm, reddish light, those well-placed blue highlights and reflecting surfaces (mirrors, plates, oblong window-panes) you think of as belonging to Dutch genre paintings; and like them it is realistic in detail and slightly sentimental. Or at least it has an aura of sentiment. (Already I'm having moments of muted grief over those of my daughter's baby clothes which are too small for her to wear any more. I will be a keeper of hair, I will store things in trunks, I will weep over photos.) But above all it's solid, everything here has solidity. No more of those washes of light, those shifts, nebulous effects of cloud, Turner sunsets, vague fears, the impalpables Jeanie used to concern herself with.

I call this woman Jeanie after the song. I can't remember any more of the song, only the title. The point (for in language there are always these "points," these reflections; this is what makes it so rich and sticky, this is why so many have disappeared beneath its dark and shining surface, why you should never try to see your own reflection in it; you will lean over too far, a strand of your hair will fall in and come out gold, and, thinking it is gold all the way down, you yourself will follow, sliding into those outstretched arms, towards the mouth you think is opening to pronounce your name but instead, just before your ears fill with pure sound, will form a word you have never heard before....)

The point, for me, is in the hair. My own hair is not light brown, but Jeanie's was. This is one difference between us. The other point is the dreaming; for Jeanie isn't real in the same way that I am real. But by now, and I mean your time, both of us will have the same degree of reality, we will be equal: wraiths, echoes, reverberations in your own brain. At the moment though Jeanie is to me as I will someday be to you. So she is real enough.

Jeanie is on her way to the hospital, to give birth, to be delivered. She is not quibbling over these terms. She's sitting in the back seat of the car, with her eyes closed and her coat spread over her like a blanket. She is doing her breathing exercises and timing her contractions with a stopwatch. She has been up since two-thirty in the morning, when she took a bath and ate some lime Jell-O, and it's now almost ten. She has learned to count, during the slow breathing, in numbers (from one to ten while breathing in, from ten to one while breathing out) which she can actually see while she is silently pronouncing them. Each number is a different color and, if she's concentrating very hard, a different typeface. They range from plain roman to ornamented circus numbers, red with gold filigree and dots. This is a refinement not mentioned in any of the numerous books she's read on the subject. Jeanie is a devotee of handbooks. She has at least two shelves of books that cover everything from building kitchen cabinets to auto repairs to smoking your own hams.

She doesn't do many of these things, but she does some of them, and in her suitcase, along with a washcloth, a package of lemon Life Savers, a pair of glasses, a hot water bottle, some talcum powder and a paper bag, is the book that suggested she take along all of these things.

(By this time you may be thinking that I've invented Jeanie in order to distance myself from these experiences. Nothing could be further from the truth. I am, in fact, trying to bring myself closer to something that time has already made distant. As for Jeanie, my intention is simple: I am bringing her back to life.)

There are two other people in the car with Jeanie. One is a man, whom I will call A., for convenience. A. is driving. When Jeanie opens her eyes, at the end of every contraction, she can see the back of his slightly balding head and his reassuring shoulders. A. drives well and not too quickly. From time to time he asks her how she is, and she tells him how long the contractions are lasting and how long there is between them. When they stop for gas he buys them each a Styrofoam container of coffee. For months he has helped her with the breathing exercises, pressing on her knee as recommended by the book, and he will be present at the delivery. (Perhaps it's to him that the birth will be given, in the same sense that one gives a performance.) Together they have toured the hospital maternity ward, in company with a small group of other pairs like them: one thin solicitous person, one slow bulbous person. They have been shown the rooms, shared and private, the sitz baths, the delivery room itself, which gave the impression of being white. The nurse was light-brown, with limber hips and elbows; she laughed a lot as she answered questions.

"First they'll give you an enema. You know what it is?

They take a tube of water and put it up your behind. Now, the gentlemen must put on this—and these, over your shoes. And these hats, this one for those with long hair, this for those with short hair."

"What about those with no hair?" says A.

The nurse looks up at his head and laughs. "Oh, you still have some," she says. "If you have a question, do not be afraid to ask."

They have also seen the film made by the hospital, a full-color film of a woman giving birth to, can it be a baby? "Not all babies will be this large at birth," the Australian nurse who introduces the movie says. Still, the audience, half of which is pregnant, doesn't look very relaxed when the lights go on. ("If you don't like the visuals," a friend of Jeanie's has told her, "you can always close your eyes.") It isn't the blood so much as the brownish-red disinfectant that bothers her. "I've decided to call this whole thing off," she says to A., smiling to show it's a joke. He gives her a hug and says, "Everything's going to be fine."

And she knows it is. Everything will be fine. But there is another woman in the car. She's sitting in the front seat, and she hasn't turned or acknowledged Jeanie in any way. She, like Jeanie, is going to the hospital. She too is pregnant. She is not going to the hospital to give birth, however, because the words, the words, are too alien to her experience, the experience she is about to have, to be used about it at all. She's wearing a cloth coat with checks in maroon and brown, and she has a kerchief tied over her hair. Jeanie has seen her before, but she knows little about her except that she is a woman who did not wish to become pregnant, who did not choose to divide herself like this, who did not choose any of these ordeals, these initiations. It would be no use telling her that everything is going to be fine. The word in English for unwanted intercourse is rape. But there is no word in the language for what is about to happen to this woman.

Jeanie has seen this woman from time to time throughout her pregnancy, always in the same coat, always with the same kerchief. Naturally, being pregnant herself has made her more aware of other pregnant women, and she has watched them, examined them covertly, every time she has seen one. But not every other pregnant woman is this woman. She did not, for instance, attend Jeanie's prenatal classes at the hospital, where the women were all young, younger than Jeanie.

"How many will be breast-feeding?" asks the Australian nurse with the hefty shoulders.

All hands but one shoot up. A modern group, the new generation, and the one lone bottle-feeder, who might have (who knows?) something wrong with her breasts, is ashamed of herself. The others look politely away from her. What they want most to discuss, it seems, are the differences between one kind of disposable diaper and another. Sometimes they lie on mats and squeeze each other's hands, simulating contractions and counting breaths. It's all very hopeful. The Australian nurse tells them not to get in and out of the bathtub by themselves. At the end of an hour they are each given a glass of apple juice.

There is only one woman in the class who has already given birth. She's there, she says, to make sure they give her a shot this time. They delayed it last time and she went through hell. The others look at her with mild disapproval. *They* are not clamoring for shots, they do not intend to go through hell. Hell comes from the wrong attitude, they feel. The books talk about *discomfort*.

"It's not discomfort, it's pain, baby," the woman says.

The others smile uneasily and the conversation slides back to disposable diapers.

Vitaminized, conscientious, well-read Jeanie, who has managed to avoid morning sickness, varicose veins, stretch marks, toxemia and depression, who has had no aberrations of appetite, no blurrings of vision—why is she followed, then, by this other? At first it was only a glimpse now and then, at the infants' clothing section in Simpson's Basement, in the supermarket lineup, on street corners as she herself slid by in A.'s car: the haggard face, the bloated torso, the kerchief holding back the too-sparse hair. In any case, it was Jeanie who saw her, not the other way around. If she knew she was following Jeanie she gave no sign.

As Jeanie has come closer and closer to this day, the unknown day on which she will give birth, as time has thickened around her so that it has become something she must propel herself through, a kind of slush, wet earth underfoot, she has seen this woman more and more often, though always from a distance. Depending on the light, she has appeared by turns as a young girl of perhaps twenty to an older woman of forty or forty-five, but there was never any doubt in Jeanie's mind that it was the same woman. In fact it did not occur to her that the woman was not real in the usual sense (and perhaps she was, originally, on the first or second sighting, as the voice that causes an echo is real), until A. stopped for a red light during this drive to the hospital and the woman, who had been standing on the corner with a brown paper bag in her arms, simply opened the front door of the car and got in. A. didn't react, and Jeanie knows better than to say anything to him. She is aware that the woman is not really there: Jeanie is not crazy. She could even make the woman disappear by opening her eyes wider, by staring, but it is only the shape that would go away, not the feeling. Jeanie isn't exactly afraid of this woman. She is afraid for her.

When they reach the hospital, the woman gets out of the car and is through the door by the time A. has come around to help Jeanie out of the back seat. In the lobby she is nowhere to be seen. Jeanie goes through Admission in the usual way, unshadowed.

There has been an epidemic of babies during the night and the maternity ward is overcrowded. Jeanie waits for her room behind a dividing screen. Nearby someone is screaming, screaming and mumbling between screams in what sounds like a foreign language. Portuguese, Jeanie thinks. She tells herself that for them it is different, you're supposed to scream, you're regarded as queer if you don't scream, it's a required part of giving birth. Nevertheless she knows that the woman screaming is the other woman and she is screaming from pain. Jeanie listens to the other voice, also a woman's, comforting, reassuring: her mother? A nurse?

A. arrives and they sit uneasily, listening to the screams. Finally Jeanie is sent for and she goes for her prep. Prep school, she thinks. She takes off her clothes—when will she see them again?—and puts on the hospital gown. She is examined, labelled around the wrist and given an enema. She tells the nurse she can't take Demerol because she's allergic to it, and the nurse writes this down. Jeanie doesn't know whether this is true or not but she doesn't want Demerol, she has read the books. She intends to put up a struggle over her pubic hair—surely she will lose her strength if it is all shaved off—but it turns out the nurse doesn't have very strong feelings about it. She is told her contractions are not far enough along to be taken seriously, she can even have lunch. She puts on her dressing gown and rejoins A., in the freshly vacated room, eats some tomato soup and a veal cutlet, and decides to take a nap while A. goes out for supplies.

Jeanie wakes up when A. comes back. He has brought a paper, some detective novels for Jeanie and a bottle of Scotch for himself. A. reads the paper and drinks Scotch, and Jeanie reads *Poirot's Early Cases.* There is no connection between Poirot and her labor, which is now intensifying, unless it is the egg-shape of Poirot's head and the vegetable marrows he is known to cultivate with strands of wet wool (placentae? umbilical cords?). She is glad the stories are short; she is walking around the room now, between contractions. Lunch was definitely a mistake.

"I think I have back labor," she says to A. They get out the handbook and look up the instructions for this. It's useful that everything has a name. Jeanie kneels on the bed and rests her forehead on her arms while A. rubs her back. A. pours himself another Scotch, in the hospital glass. The nurse, in pink, comes, looks, asks about the timing, and goes away again. Jeanie is beginning to sweat. She can only manage half a page or so of Poirot before she has to clamber back up on the bed again and begin breathing and running through the colored numbers.

When the nurse comes back, she has a wheelchair. It's time to go down to the labor room, she says. Jeanie feels stupid sitting in the wheelchair. She tells herself about peasant women having babies in the fields, Indian women having them on portages with hardly a second thought. She feels effete. But the hospital wants her to ride, and considering the fact that the nurse is tiny, perhaps it's just as well. What if Jeanie were to collapse, after all? After all her courageous talk. An image of the tiny pink nurse, antlike, trundling large Jeanie through the corridors, rolling her along like a heavy beach ball.

As they go by the check-in desk a woman is wheeled past on a table, covered by a sheet. Her eyes are closed and there's a bottle feeding into her arm through a tube. Something is wrong. Jeanie looks back—she thinks it was the other woman—but the sheeted table is hidden now behind the counter.

In the dim labor room Jeanie takes off her dressing gown and is helped up onto the bed by the nurse. A. brings her suitcase, which is not a suitcase actually but a small flight bag, the significance of this has not been lost on Jeanie, and in fact she now has some of the apprehensive feelings she associates with planes, including the fear of a crash. She takes out her Life Savers, her glasses, her washcloth and the other things she thinks she will need. She removes her contact lenses and places them in their case, reminding A. that they must not be lost. Now she is purblind.

There is something else in her bag that she doesn't remove. It's a talisman, given to her several years ago as a souvenir by a travelling friend of hers. It's a rounded oblong of opaque blue glass, with four yellow-and-white eye shapes on it. In Turkey, her friend has told her, they hang them on mules to protect against the Evil Eye. Jeanie knows this talisman probably won't work for her, she is not Turkish and she isn't a mule, but it makes her feel safer to have it in the room with her. She had planned to hold it in her hand during the most difficult part of labor but somehow there is no longer any time for carrying out plans like this.

An old woman, a fat old woman dressed all in green, comes into the room and sits beside Jeanie. She says to A., who is sitting on the other side of Jeanie, "That is a good watch. They don't make watches like that any more." She is referring to his gold pocket watch, one of his few extravagances, which is on the night table. Then she places her hand on Jeanie's belly to feel the contraction. "This is good," she says, her accent is Swedish or German. "This, I call a contraction. Before, it was nothing." Jeanie can no longer remember having seen her before. "Good. Good."

"When will I have it?" Jeanie asks, when she can talk, when she is no longer counting.

The old woman laughs. Surely that laugh, those tribal hands, have presided over a thousand beds, a thousand kitchen tables... "A long time yet," she says. "Eight, ten hours."

"But I've been *doing* this for twelve hours already," Jeanie says.

"Not hard labor," the woman says. "Not good, like this."

Jeanie settles into herself for the long wait. At the moment she can't remember why she wanted to have a baby in the first place. That decision was made by someone else, whose motives are now unclear. She remembers the way women who had babies used to smile at one another, mysteriously, as if there was something they knew that she didn't, the way they would casually exclude her from their frame of reference. What was the knowledge, the mystery, or was having a baby really no more inexplicable than having a car accident or an orgasm? (But these too were indescribable, events of the body, all of them; why should the mind distress itself trying to find a language for them?) She has sworn she will never do that to any woman without children, engage in those passwords and exclusions. She's old enough, she's been put through enough years of it to find it tiresome and cruel.

But—and this is the part of Jeanie that goes with the talisman hidden in her bag, not with the part that longs to build kitchen cabinets and smoke hams—she is, secretly, hoping for a mystery. Something more than this, something else, a vision. After all she is risking her life, though it's not too likely she will die. Still, some women do. Internal bleeding, shock, heart failure, a mistake on the part of someone, a nurse, a doctor. She deserves a vision, she deserves to be allowed to bring something back with her from this dark place into which she is now rapidly descending.

She thinks momentarily about the other woman. Her motives, too, are unclear. Why doesn't she want to have a baby? Has she been raped, does she have ten other children, is she starving? Why hasn't she had an abortion? Jeanie doesn't know, and in fact it no longer matters why. *Uncross your fingers,* Jeanie thinks to her. Her face, distorted with pain and terror, floats briefly behind Jeanie's eyes before it too drifts away.

Jeanie tries to reach down to the baby, as she has many times before, sending waves of love, color, music, down through her arteries to it, but she finds she can no longer do this. She can no longer feel the baby as a baby, its arms and legs poking, kicking, turning. It has collected itself together, it's a hard sphere, it does not have time right now to listen to her. She's grateful for this because she isn't sure anyway how good the message would be. She no longer has control of the numbers either, she can no longer see them, although she continues mechanically to count. She realizes she has practised for the wrong thing, A. squeezing her knee was nothing, she should have practised for this, whatever it is.

"Slow down," A. says. She's on her side now, he's holding her hand. "Slow it right down."

"I can't, I can't do it, I can't do this."

"Yes, you can."

"Will I sound like that?"

"Like what?" A. says. Perhaps he can't hear it: it's the other woman, in the room next door or the room next door to that. She's screaming and crying, screaming and crying. While she cries she is saying, over and over, "It hurts. It hurts."

"No, you won't," he says. So there is someone, after all.

A doctor comes in, not her own doctor. They want her to turn over on her back.

"I can't," she says. "I don't like it that way." Sounds have receded, she has trouble hearing them. She turns over and the doctor gropes with her rubber-gloved hand. Something wet and hot flows over her thighs.

"It was just ready to break," the doctor says. "All I had to do was touch it. Four centimetres," she says to A.

"Only *four?*" Jeanie says. She feels cheated; they must be wrong. The doctor says her own doctor will be called in time. Jeanie is outraged at them. They have not understood, but it's too late to say this and she slips back into the dark place, which is not hell, which is more like being inside, trying to get out. *Out*, she says or thinks. Then she is floating, the numbers are gone, if anyone told her to get up, go out of the room, stand on her head, she would do it. From minute to minute she comes up again, grabs for air.

"You're hyperventilating," A. says. "Slow it down." He is rubbing her back now, hard, and she takes his hand and shoves it viciously further down, to the right place, which is not the right place as soon as his hand is there. She remembers a story she read once, about the Nazis tying the legs of Jewish women together during labor. She never really understood before how that could kill you.

A nurse appears with a needle. "I don't want it," Jeanie says.

"Don't be hard on yourself," the nurse says. "You don't have to go through pain like that." What pain? Jeanie thinks. When there is no pain she feels nothing, when there is pain, she feels nothing because there is no *she.* This, finally, is the disappearance of language. *You don't remember afterwards,* she has been told by almost everyone.

Jeanie comes out of a contraction, gropes for control. "Will it hurt the baby?" she says.

"It's a mild analgesic," the doctor says. "We wouldn't allow anything that would hurt the baby." Jeanie doesn't believe this. Nevertheless she is jabbed, and the doctor is right, it is very mild, because it doesn't seem to do a thing for Jeanie, though A. later tells her she has slept briefly between contractions.

Suddenly she sits bolt upright. She is wide awake and lucid. "You have to ring that bell right now," she says. "This baby is being born."

A. clearly doesn't believe her. "I can feel it, I can feel the head," she says. A. pushes the button for the call bell. A nurse appears and checks, and now everything is happening too soon, nobody is ready. They set off down the hall, the nurse wheeling Jeanie feels fine. She watches the corridors, the edges of everything shadowy because she doesn't have her glasses on. She hopes A. will remember to bring them. They pass another doctor.

"Need me?" she asks.

"Oh no," the nurse answers breezily. "Natural childbirth."

Jeanie realizes that this woman must have been the

anaesthetist. "What?" she says, but it's too late now, they are in the room itself, all those glossy surfaces, tubular strange apparatus like a science-fiction movie, and the nurse is telling her to get onto the delivery table. No one else is in the room.

"You must be crazy," Jeanie says.

"Don't push," the nurse says.

"What do you mean?" Jeanie says. This is absurd. Why should she wait, why should the baby wait for them because they're late?

"Breathe through your mouth," the nurse says. "Pant," and Jeanie finally remembers how. When the contraction is over she uses the nurse's arm as a lever and hauls herself across onto the table.

From somewhere her own doctor materializes, in her doctor suit already, looking even more like Mary Poppins than usual, and Jeanie says, "Bet you weren't expecting to see me so soon!" The baby is being born when Jeanie said it would, though just three days ago the doctor said it would be at least another week, and this makes Jeanie feel jubilant and smug. Not that she knew, she'd believed the doctor.

She's being covered with a green tablecloth, they are taking far too long, she feels like pushing the baby out now, before they are ready. A. is there by her head, swathed in robes, hats, masks. He has forgotten her glasses. "Push now," the doctor says. Jeanie grips with her hands, grits her teeth, face, her whole body together, a snarl, a fierce smile, the baby is enormous, a stone, a boulder, her bones unlock, and, once, twice, the third time, she opens like a birdcage turning slowly inside out.

A pause; a wet kitten slithers between her legs. "Why don't you look?" says the doctor, but Jeanie still has her eyes closed. No glasses, she couldn't have seen a thing anyway. "Why don't you look?" the doctor says again.

Jeanie opens her eyes. She can see the baby, who has been wheeled up beside her and is fading already from the alarming birth purple. A good baby, she thinks, meaning it as the old woman did: *a good watch*, well-made, substantial. The baby isn't crying; she squints in the new light. Birth isn't something that has been given to her, nor has she taken it. It was just something that has happened so they could greet each other like this. The nurse is stringing beads for her name. When the baby is bundled and tucked beside Jeanie, she goes to sleep.

As for the vision, there wasn't one. Jeanie is conscious of no special knowledge; already she's forgetting what it was like. She's tired and very cold; she is shaking, and asks for another blanket. A. comes back to the room with her; her clothes are still there. Everything is quiet, the other woman is no longer screaming. Something has happened to her, Jeanie knows. Is she dead? Is the baby dead? Perhaps she is one of those casualties (and how can Jeanie herself be sure, yet, that she will not be among them) who will go into postpartum depression and never come out. "You see, there was nothing to be afraid of," A. says before he leaves, but he was wrong.

The next morning Jeanie wakes up when it's light. She's been warned about getting out of bed the first time without the help of a nurse, but she decides to do it anyway (peasant in the field! Indian on the portage!). She's still running adrenaline, she's also weaker than she thought, but she wants very much to look out the window. She feels she's been inside too long, she wants to see the sun come up. Being awake this early always makes her feel a little unreal, a little insubstantial, as if she's partly transparent, partly dead.

(It was to me, after all, that the birth was given, Jeanie gave it, I am the result. What would she make of me? Would she be pleased?)

The window is two panes with a venetian blind sandwiched between them; it turns by a knob at the side. Jeanie has never seen a window like this before. She closes and opens the blind several times. Then she leaves it open and looks out.

All she can see from the window is a building. It's an old stone building, heavy and Victorian, with a copper roof oxidized to green. It's solid, hard, darkened by soot, dour, leaden. But as she looks at this building, so old and seemingly immutable, she sees that it's made of water. Water, and some tenuous jelly-like substance. Light flows through it from behind (the sun is coming up), the building is so thin, so fragile, that it quivers in the slight dawn wind. Jeanie sees that if the building is this way (a touch could destroy it, a ripple of the earth, why has no one noticed, guarded it against accidents?) then the rest of the world must be like this too, the entire earth, the rocks, people, trees, everything needs to be protected, cared for, tended. The enormity of this task defeats her; she will never be up to it, and what will happen then?

Jeanie hears footsteps in the hall outside her door. She thinks it must be the other woman, in her brown-and-maroon-checked coat, carrying her paper bag, leaving the hospital now that her job is done. She has seen Jeanie safely through, she must go now to hunt through the streets of the city for her next case. But the door opens, it's a nurse, who is just in time to catch Jeanie as she sinks to the floor, holding on to the edge of the air-conditioning unit. The nurse scolds her for getting up too soon.

After that the baby is carried in, solid, substantial, packed together like an apple, Jeanie examines her, she is complete, and in the days that follow Jeanie herself becomes drifted over with new words, her hair slowly darkens, she ceases to be what she was and is replaced, gradually, by someone else.

Colors

Sylvia A. Watanabe

"Last night I went dream," Little Grandma said, laying the blue volcano next to the red and yellow hula girls. "I dreamed I saw the hungry ghosts coming home across the water...."

Little Grandma was always having dreams. She said the spirits of our kin watched from the shrine on her bedroom bureau and spoke to her while she was sleeping. She said they told her of sickness and family troubles, and where to hunt when Cousin Makoto misplaced his store teeth, and what chicken to bet on at the chicken fights.

Every few months, even years after I left the island to live on the East Coast, I'd be startled awake at three in the morning by the ringing of the telephone. It was Little Grandma calling long distance. "Last night I went dream," her voice would chirp into the sleep-heavy silence. "I dreamed I saw your face...."

"Tell her it can wait," my husband Ben would grumble, reaching toward me and drawing sleep close again.

Outside, it always seemed to be winter, and I secretly cherished the sound of her voice. As I dozed with the receiver close to my ear, the colors of the island would crowd into the darkness behind my eyes—the green of the canefields, the rust-colored earth, the sea....

Green, red, blue. The silver pins glinted in Little Grandma's hands, as she laid the patchwork triangles, one by one, into the shapes of stars. The gold cap on her front tooth gleamed. She seemed all tiny glints and flashes, like light shining through a creaky door.

"In my dream, it was night," she said. "There was no moon—only black, the sky was; black the ocean...." She looked up from her piecing and gestured toward the resort complex across the bay. "All over there, where the hotel is now, there was only sand."

The scent of Three Flowers Brilliantine and stale urine drifted toward me from Papa dozing in his lawn chair. As he breathed, he made a sound like waves hissing out across the sand. A delicate stream trickled from the corner of his mouth.

"Come see!" I could hear him calling....

I opened my sketchpad.

..."Hana, come see!", and once again, I was running toward the sound. As I drew close, he held his finger to his lips. "Shhh ... there...." And he pointed to the crown flower hedge alive with monarch butterflies or the mango tree where a mother cardinal was teaching her babies to fly....

During the last five or six years, the "forgetting sickness," as Little Grandma called it, had gradually stolen the names of things from him, 'til only his eyes remained alive in his face, seeing and seeing. My visits home grew more infrequent and were finally replaced by telephoned regrets—Ben had a touch of the flu, we were on deadline at the office....

Now, I could feel the silence seeping out of Papa, as he slept, swallowing words I hadn't spoken, drawing everything into itself, like a great hunger.

Across the yard, the summer quilt on the clothesline rippled like a sail opening in the wind. The late afternoon sun glimmered through the poinsiana above us—red, gold—across the whiteness of Papa's sleeping face, the whiteness of the sketchpad lying open on my lap.

"Then, from far away," Little Grandma was saying, "the sky began changing colors, the ocean was shining...."

Aunt Pearlie put down her newspaper and gave me a see-what-I-mean look. "We heard this yesterday, I think...."

Grandma turned the patchwork star in her hands, pinning it to a square of blue cotton. "The ocean was shining...."

Aunty took a sip of iced tea, then held up the article she'd been reading. Her lips left angry scarlet kisses around the rim of her glass. Rise in Sex Crimes, the headline said.

"Nothing's sacred anymore," she grumbled. "A woman's not safe in her own bed—not even here in this very village...."

Aunt Pearlie, my father's younger sister, taught kindergarten at the Jesus Coming Soon Japanese Missionary School in Honolulu. She had never married. The only time she'd ever visited Ben and me in New York, she'd wakened at least twice every night to check the locks on the front door. After staying less than a week, she'd finally decided to cancel the next two weeks of her visit; she couldn't take the loss of sleep, she said.

"Just the other day," Aunt Pearlie continued, "I was talking to Emiko McAllister over at the Koyama Store...."

Little Grandma got up and threw her shawl lightly across Papa's shoulders. "Ko-chan," she whispered. "You're going to catch cold, if you sleep with your mouth open."

He mumbled sleepily in his sleep.

Aunt Pearlie raised her voice. "And Emi told me that she'd heard that the Laundry Burglar is on the loose again!"

Little Grandma settled back in her chair, then turned toward me. "Where was I, Hana-chan?"

"It turns my blood cold..." Pearlie hugged herself and rubbed her upper arms with her hands "...to think of Someone Like That sneaking around our backyards and doing God knows what to our clean laundry!"

Grandma ignored her. "Hana, do you remember?"

"Oh, Mama!" Pearlie almost shouted. "Something about the ocean, for Pete's sake!"

"Yes. So datta." Grandma laid down her piecing and looked out across the bay. "Akarukute, akarukute ... the lights became bright and more bright, close and more close...."

"Then, what?" I asked

"Then, I woke up."

"What?" Pearlie said.

"That's all."

"What kind of a dream is that?"

Little Grandma serenely resumed her piecing. Pin, turn. Each movement fit into the next, like a perfectly-made seam. "It wasn't just a dream. It's how the hungry ghosts come home every year at O-bon time, when we are asleep."

Aunt Pearlie pressed her lips together and frowned at her newspaper.

Pin, turn. Watching Little Grandma, you couldn't imagine any other way of piecing a quilt. I looked down the hill at the cloud shadows moving like dream across the sugar fields. Pin, turn. Land curving into sea into sky.

"How come you like New York so much, Hana?" Little Grandma asked. Her voice softened. "It's so far ... everybody has gone so far. You in New York. Pearlie in Honolulu. Ko-chan in ... ano ... ano ... tokoro...." That place, she called it; she avoided the words, hospital, nursing home.

She looked around at us, and her face cleared. "Ureshii ..." She smiled. "Grandpa will be so happy when he comes home at O-bon, and sees that all of you are here again."

The annual Festival of the Dead would begin in a few days. Already, the scaffolding for the musician's platform had been built in front of the temple, the lanterns strung around the yard. Every festival season since grandfather's death, Little Grandma had faithfully put out the ritual servings of ghost food and rice wine to celebrate his brief return. And on the last night of the festival, when the spirits went back across the sea, she'd carried a paper lantern down to the water to light him on his way.

Aunt Pearlie turned the page of her paper, then crisply swatted the crease down the middle. "There's no need for anyone to be lonely. I keep telling her to come and live with me..."

Papa sat up and rubbed his eyes.

"...But there's no such thing as reasoning with some people."

I rose to go to him, the box of crayons spilling from my lap onto the grass. Aunty waved at me to sit down again, then stood and held out her hands to him. "Come, Brother. It's time to wash up." She glanced at me. "Like I said, there's no such thing as reasoning with them."

"I'm hungry," Papa said.

Aunt Pearlie took his hand. "First, we wash; then, we can have some cake and juice."

"Ureshii...." Grandma said, as we watched them shamble toward the house.

·

The week before, I'd been wakened in the early morning by the ringing of the telephone. It had been about two months since Ben had moved out. Even half-asleep, I missed his warmth beside me, the sound of his voice mumbling sleepy protests in the dark. In the tiny confrontations with nothingness that occurred, like this, at a hundred odd times in a day, the pattern of our life together was becoming unmade—the old patchwork falling away into incoherent fragments of color, into no-color, into blackness.

R-r-r-ing. It was midnight, according to the alarm clock next to the bed. Too early for Grandma. Besides, she'd called the week before—to relay another of her dreams, her way of reminding me that O-bon was coming up and maybe I should think of returning for the tenth year observance of Grandfather's death. I said I'd think about it, unable to tell her about Ben, whom she'd always regarded as a "tanin," an outsider.

R-r-r-ing. Perhaps it was Ben, now. What would I say? My hands trembled as I picked up the receiver. "Hello?"

"Hana, where have you been, oh my God...."

It was Aunt Pearlie.

"Uh ... hi Aunty. I was sleeping."

"Poor baby, I forgot about the time. Actually, I would never have called, except I've been at Grandma's the last week ... and ... you know how she is. She won't listen to me. You've got to come home. Talk some sense into her."

I struggled to grasp what she was not saying. It took too much effort. I began to feel annoyed. "Well, it's not exactly like crossing the street...."

"You'll never guess what she's gone and done now!"

Her alarm was beginning to be contagious. "What's happened?"

"Week before last, the Director of the Aloha Nani Nursing Home called me in Honolulu...."

"Papa? Something's happened to Papa?" He'd been staying at the Home ever since Grandma had fallen and sprained her hip the previous summer.

"Your Grandmother has stolen him out of there and won't give him back!"

The next day, I took a leave of absence from the design studio where I worked, closed my apartment, and caught a late night flight from Kennedy.

The row of finished morning star squares glowed like colored windows, as Little Grandma held them to the light. The sun shining through them cast red, and violet, and orange reflections across her face, and I could no longer see the structure of the bone and flesh beneath the shifting surface of color. Planes had become hollows; hollows, planes. I laid my crayon down, the page before me empty.

That night, I dreamed again of the waves. The dream never changed. The darkness. The empty beach. The rumbling of the ocean, like a great engine, drawing closer and closer in the dark. As I turned in the direction of the water, I could see the black shapes of the waves, tall as mountains against the sky. The rumbling grew louder. I scrambled for the sand bank behind me and began to climb. The sand slid away beneath my feet. The rumbling became a roar....

Papa's snoring filled the house. At first, I half-dreamed I was back in New York with Ben. "Shh, shh," I murmured, turning over. The moonlight streamed onto my face through the open curtains across the room.

As I blinked awake, I recognized the mahogany toy cabinet with the china tea set sitting on top, the red wooden child's rocker, Papa's paintings of birds and animals upon the walls. Here and there in the moonlight, a tangerine-colored bear or a lavender parrot sprang from the shadows in a vivid flash of color. The darkness was permeated with the smell of linseed oil and fresh paint.

The snoring quieted.

"Akai tori, ko tori," Little Grandma was singing upstairs in the attic. "Red bird, little red bird, why are you so red?" As she paused for breath, I could hear the crisp sound of her sewing shears, snipping patchwork.

"We'll all be in a nursing home before she finishes that thing," Aunt Pearlie said the next afternoon, as we sat at the kitchen table, eating slices of chilled mango and looking out the window at Little Grandma and Papa under the poinsiana tree. "She's been at that same quilt for the past four years, I'd swear. Did you hear her last night? I tell you, between the singing and the snoring...."

"But we can't make her take him back," I said.

"We can't go on like this—that's what we can't do!

Besides, what'll Ben think, you being gone so long?"

"Ben?" I reached for another slice of mango, took a bite, chewed. I shrugged. "He'll manage, I guess...."

"But that's not the point, Hana...."

It's not that I don't love you, he'd said.

"I feel bad, we all feel bad about your Papa...."

...But I've stopped growing....

"Life goes on, after all!" Aunt Pearlie cried.

Bright, dark. The morning light flickered across the walls. The contours of the room shifted, as the boundaries between shapes melted, and colors slid away into shadow. Everything was sliding, sliding....

"If Grandma were by herself, she could sell this place, come and stay with me...."

The sea rumbled faintly. I squeezed my eyes closed, as if that would help me to shut out the sound.

"You know the real estate company that built the hotel across the bay? Well, one of the developers dropped by the other day...."

Hana, come see!

"...He said they were interested in buying all the land around this area, putting up a shopping mall...."

I remembered the sound of Papa's voice, guiding my hands, as I learned to mix colors. "How do you make red redder?" he'd ask. "How many different kinds of black can you see?" The rumbling died away.

"Look, Hana," Aunt Pearlie said. "We've got to be practical about this situation...."

Emi McAllister, our next-door neighbor, had let herself in the front gate and was coming up the walk. She was carrying what looked like a dish or tray wrapped in a grocery bag.

"What's she got there?" Aunt Pearlie reached for her

spectacles in her apron pocket and put them on. "Hmmm. Probably some of that brown fudge that sticks to the roof of your mouth." She started for the door. "Or some of those hard little puffed rice cakes."

Emi stopped to talk to Little Grandma, then looked up and waved to Aunty.

"Oh, rice cakes," Aunt Pearlie said, taking the bag as Emi came up the front porch steps into the house.

Emi had just come from working in her garden and carried the smell of fresh air and sunlight into the kitchen. "Just a little welcome home for Hana." She smiled at me. "Your Papa's looking fine."

Dark, bright. The colors sliding. "You think so? I guess."

"Well, he's not fine." Aunt Pearlie offered the dish of cakes to Emi. "I've been trying to talk some sense into this girl. She's as bad as her grandmother."

"I didn't say he shouldn't go back," I protested. "I said we couldn't force Grandma into taking him...."

Emi waved aside the cakes. "Never touch 'em, too hard on my old teeth." She patted my hand. "Things going badly, huh?"

Aunt Pearlie frowned. "So, Emi, how're you doing? Heard any more news about the Laundry Burglar?"

During the last several summers, the village had been plagued by brief outbreaks of laundry burglaries which never followed any particular pattern and never went on for more than two or three weeks at a time. In the past, missing items had included the scarf from Emi's gardening hat, a pair of Doc McAllister's running shorts, the pink rose from Cousin Missy's scholarship dress ... nothing, however, had ever been found missing from Aunt Pearlie's wash.

"Mrs. Koyama says the dancing school teacher is missing her white satin night cap." Emi reached for a slice of mango. "Everyone knows that woman wears a wig...."

"It's disgraceful that this situation has been allowed to go on for so long!" Aunt Pearlie interrupted. "Who knows what a twisted mind like that will do next?"

"You have to admit, he hasn't done much of anything in the last four or five years," Emi pointed out.

"He's probably just testing the waters, that's all. We've been lulled into a false sense of security."

Emi put the last of the mango into her mouth. "It's true, no one can ever really know what anyone else is thinking."

"It's about time the police began doing their jobs!"

Emi sighed. "From what I hear, the sheriff doesn't have much to go on. The burglaries always stop before any real clues turn up."

"Meantime, what's a person to do? You don't know how I worry ... my mother out here all alone...."

Emi clucked sympathetically.

"Look at this place! It's just too much—especially after she sprained her hip last summer. And with Brother the way he is, you've got to keep your eye on him every minute. Every minute. When I came to stay with my mother after her accident—you should have seen me I was going crazy with the two of them—I was so exhausted, I used to fall asleep on my feet. One afternoon, I must have dropped off, and the next thing I knew, the vegetable man was knocking at the door—he was bringing Brother back, he said, he found him wandering the road to the upcountry about three miles outside the village...."

"That's odd...." Emi was looking out the window.

"...That's when I decided that the best thing for

Brother...."

Emi turned toward Aunt Pearlie. "...I was just talking to your mother out there a minute ago."

Aunty and I looked out too.

The quilting mat was still spread out under the poinsiana, but the wind had blown the cover off a shoebox full of piecing and was scattering the bright scraps across the grass. Neither Little Grandma nor Papa was anywhere to be seen.

"Papa!" I called, scanning the rocks and tidal pools along the shore. The sky and sea were the color of fire. A wave broke over the lava shelf and came swirling around my ankles. I had to hurry. The tide was rising and the way to the point would soon be under water. "Papa!"

Shortly after we'd discovered them missing, Little Grandma had come limping up the road to the house. "Hayaku! Call Sheriff Kanoi! Ko-chan has run away!" she panted.

On a hunch, I'd slipped away to the beach, while Aunt Pearlie got on the phone to the police. In my childhood, Papa had taken me out to the point almost every weekend in fine weather. At first, he'd bring along his painting things, but he'd always forget the time as he stood working on his canvas, and we'd end up staying out too long. Once, he lost an easel when he tried to cross back to shore as the tide was coming in. After that, we took walks to the point "just for look," as Little Grandma put it.

We watched for whales in winter—each of us vying to be first to spot the beautiful white plumes of spray, rising above the waves. He taught me the names of the sea plants growing among the rocks and how to identify the schools of fish, flashing just beneath the surface of the water. A green flash for manini. Silver for papio.

The waves were washing higher and higher upon the lava shelf. The red in the sky had deepened.

"Papa!" I called, raging against time which gave us everything—all love, all beauty—only to steal them back again.

Then, I saw him. A speck of white at the end of the point. I picked my way across the jagged rocks, the waves crashing higher and higher, until I was wading through knee-deep water toward him. "You've scared us all to death," I scolded, as I pulled myself up beside him.

He turned toward me, his face transfixed. "See, Hana," he said. "Oh, see." He gestured toward the glittering path of red and gold, leading from where he stood, across the water, to the sun.

"I just turned my back for one second...." Little Grandma was explaining again to Aunt Pearlie downstairs in the kitchen, as I drew the water for Papa's bath.

"That's why I keep telling you...." Aunt Pearlie replied.

Papa sat shivering on the toilet seat, watching me.

"Just a minute and I'll help you out of those wet things," I said. "I think I know why you run away, huh, Papa?"

He had not spoken since out on the point.

"You feel something missing...."

I unbuttoned his shirt and helped him pull his arms through the sleeves.

"...It's like Ben told me once, about growing...."

I pulled Papa's T-shirt over his head.

"...well, maybe it's not the same. But we're all looking for something...."

I kneeled before him and began unlacing his shoes. I

looked into his face.

"Papa, talk to me. I heard you out there...."

"Hard-headed old woman!" Aunt Pearlie shouted. There were heavy footsteps on the stairs. A door slammed.

Papa reached for the gold chain around my neck. "Pretty," he said.

"...talk to me...." I whispered.

When I finally got to bed, I lay listening to the sounds of the house—Papa snoring, clocks ticking, the back porch door banging in the breeze, and weaving in and out, making a single song of them all, Grandmother humming upstairs in the attic.

I dreamed of the waves. Once more, I was scrambling up the sandbank, the sound of the ocean drawing close behind me. It was dark, so dark. The faster I climbed, the faster the sand slid away. The sound drew nearer, it was almost on me. I reached the top. Safe. Then, I turned. The waves were behind me.

I was wakened by the sound of silverware rattling against dishes, and cupboard doors slamming. The smell of fresh coffee filled my room.

As I walked into the kitchen, the wash was going, and there was french toast burning on the stove. "Grandma!" I turned off the range and poured myself a cup of coffee. "Grandma?"

Aunt Pearlie pushed through the back screen door, with an empty laundry basket under her arm. "I was just out hanging the wash. You want some toast?"

I shook my head. "Coffee's fine for me."

She pulled out the chair next to mine and sat staring through the window, as she clasped and unclasped her hands. Finally, she spoke. "Quite a little adventure yesterday, huh?"

"Mmm ... Do you know where Grandma is?"

"She and your father have gone to the Prayer Lady's to get a laying-on of hands, or whatever it is the woman does."

I got up and went to the stove. "Maybe I will have some toast."

"If you ask me, he needs more than a good massage to fix what's wrong with him...."

I turned and faced her. "Why do you have to keep going on and on about it?"

"Because someone has to! What are you going to do – spend the rest of your life...."

"You act as if you want him to be locked up!"

She was silent. Her hands lay, still, upon the table. There was a funny bruised look about her eyes.

"What did he ever do to you? It's not as if he were some sort of maniac!"

Her mouth was set once more in an ugly stubborn line. "Oh, isn't he? Look, Hana." She pulled something out of her apron. "Look what I found in your Papa's pants pocket!" She laid the dancing school teacher's white satin nightcap on the table.

Little Grandma took the news calmly. She agreed with no further protest that Papa should be returned to the Home. Aunt Pearlie said that he could stay until the Bon festival was over, the following day.

Pin, turn. One by one, Little Grandma laid the patchwork triangles into the shapes of stars. The late afternoon sun flickered through the poinsiana above us, casting red and gold reflections across her face. My sketchpad lay open on my lap.

Pin, turn. Aunt Pearlie snored in her lawn chair, her newspaper covering her face. Papa sat on the grass, digging at the roots of the tree.

"It's good to have everybody together," Little Grandma said.

For the first time since Ben had left, I felt the tears begin to come.

Little Grandma put aside her piecing and took my face in her hands. "Shikkari shite," she whispered. "You must be strong."

"I'll never see ... I'll never ... oh Ben...." I sobbed, "...and they'll put Papa back in there ... and he'll ... we'll never...."

"Maybe so." A sly look flickered across her face. She shrugged, then stood and walked over to Papa. She helped him to his feet and began heading toward the house. She waved at me. "Come. You come too!"

Little Grandma led us up the stairs to her room on the second floor. Inside, it was nearly bare—except for a tiny cot with a hard loaf-shaped pillow, the family shrine on the camphor wood bureau, and the tattered photographs of our dead kin which covered every wall.

"Come, come." She directed us through what looked like a closet door, leading up another narrow flight of stairs, to the attic.

She switched on the light. A quilting frame stood in one corner. In the middle of the floor lay a mat covered with little piles of geometric shapes cut from scraps of fabric. Along each wall were stacks of shoeboxes and grocery bags spilling over with bits of piecing and appliqué in various stages of completion. I recognized a blue scrap from one of Papa's old painting smocks, a yellow piece from my first going-out dress.

But it was to the far end of the attic that my eyes were drawn. On the wall, there hung an immense quilt made of appliquéd squares, separated by strips of morning stars. The quilt was not finished, but already it covered the entire back wall, from ceiling to floor. From where I stood, perhaps fifteen feet away, it seemed to contain every color in the entire world.

I moved closer, and the colors began to cohere into shapes. Each square depicted places and people in the life of the village. There were the sugar fields sloping down to the sea. The rows of identical green and white houses with a different-colored dog in each yard. There was the singing tree in the temple ground and the old head priest at O-bon, leading the procession of lights down to the bay. There was Emi McAllister in her garden. Every detail was perfect—down to the green and pink scarf on her tiny sun hat.

I looked closer. No, it couldn't be. My heart beat faster. It just couldn't. I glanced quickly over the rest of the quilt—at Doc McAllister out for his morning run, and Cousin Missy standing at the window of her Mama's house, and the Koyama Store Lady in front of her store ... it was true. There, in that quilt was every single piece of laundry missing in the village during the last four years!

Little Grandma smiled. "For not forget," she said.

I turned and walked down the stairs and out of the house, into the colors of the afternoon.

Penetrations

Jane Lazarre

They were hanging a South African poet that night. She thought about it while she dressed and drank her coffee. All over the world, protests were arranged, voices shouted in newsprint, telegrams, fruitless pleas, righteous indignation. She sat on the southbound IRT on her way to school, correcting papers, thinking about it in the pauses between one student's essay and another. His face came back to her, the dark serious face she'd seen in the *New York Times*. Deep crevices lining the cheeks. She couldn't tell from the slightly blurred photo if they were lines of age or ritual.

At 23rd Street she returned the essays to their folder and concentrated on the poet. He was ready to die for freedom, he said in a message sent from his cell. But waiting for the hangman, perhaps he was thinking of his children, or his old mother who had been haunting the prison walls for days, refusing to leave, telling the guards: Kill me if you want to. He's my son. Perhaps he cried. Perhaps he was as scared as she would be in his place. Julia began to cry.

It was not odd in itself, to cry this way about the death of a poet thousands of miles away. Many people would cry if the South African government went through with the hanging. And Julia had once been a writer too. She cried for the poet and for the power of honest language which could still frighten governments, even in this nuclear age. But in her country, books—like certain elegant plastics—had become so expensive, and few writers so valuable, that small contracts dwindled and many writers stopped writing, since they had to get jobs, raise children, and there wasn't any time left over. Julia was one of those who, for lack of time and lack of hope, had stopped.

Now, here was this poet being killed for his words. It would not have been odd for her to cry over such a thing, except that Julia had not cried over anything for several years. She wondered at her tears which flowed in fast streams down her cheeks causing other passengers to look at her uncomfortably. The woman next to her opened her black canvas bag and handed her a blue perfumed tissue. Julia nodded her appreciation and blew her nose.

The day was unusually hectic, leaving little time to think about anything besides classes, conferences with students, a faculty meeting. But there was one ten minute period, when she was on line in the cafeteria, an egg salad sandwich in one hand, a cold diet soda in the other, when the African poet's face came back to her and right there on line, just as she reached the cashier and held out her five dollar bill, she nearly cried again.

On the subway going home in the evening, Julia stood near the door, crushed between a tall man and a woman in a fur coat. She forced her eyes downward, focussing on a tiny space of floor in order to avoid leaning her forehead on the man's chest, or eating the woman's fur. Usually she was intensely aware of other bodies, other hands touching hers, preferring to risk falling than to keep her hand on a crowded pole where some man might cover her fingers and she would have to wonder if it were accident or a nasty invitation to seduction. Suddenly, though, Julia realized that two hands were sandwiching hers on the pole which she had apparently grasped, unaware. Warily, she looked up from the hands, up the arms, to the faces. One belonged to a young woman whose other arm sheltered two small children, pulling them to her side as the train rocked and bumped along the tracks. The other hand, however, belonged to an older Hispanic man whose eyes, when Julia reached them, met her own. He smiled, warmly. Glancing at the rope of hands between them, she realized he could not know her eyes belonged to the hand he pressed so firmly on the pole. She smiled back at him. And this was the second thing that happened that day which Julia knew was odd. For years, she'd felt a drumming anxiety whenever she was in the presence of strange or barely known men, so that she had learned to turn her eyes quickly from a man on the street, an acquaintance, especially if she were attracted to him. Once she had been a passionate woman. Often she would cry during sex from the sheer enormity of the pleasure of connection. But for years she'd made love with her husband, Bruce, only occasionally. She thought of it as sexual amnesia. It wasn't that she didn't want sex.

Rather, there was something she couldn't remember about sex, some aspect of desire she'd lost her knowledge of, and this loss made her unable to contemplate sex for months at a time. Yet here she was, smiling at this dark haired stranger, noticing the pleasing muscles at the base of his neck just beneath the line of the dark blue collar of his shirt.

The train emptied out somewhat at 72nd Street, but the man next to her remained, still smiling. So Julia rushed out onto the platform and entered another car further up the line. Finding a seat, she leaned against the heated plastic determined to pull herself together so she could discuss the issue of the South African poet with her children at dinner—taking care that they not be spared this most recent lesson in their moral and political education to which she paid such obsessive attention. Just as she was worrying that her younger son, Anthony, might be upset by the execution, a tall bony man walked toward her down the central aisle. He was dressed in thick, layered rags which, by now, were to all urban dwellers the sign of homelessness. But his rags were thicker than any she had seen so that while his face and hands indicated frailty, his body, layered many times with filthy sweaters and coats, appeared husky, shapeless and oddly comforting, like an old down quilt. She looked away from him, as other passengers were doing, but she felt him stop near her seat and look down at her. He did nothing, only remained before her, staring. Finally, she returned his gaze. His age could not be easily determined but Julia thought he might be young. There were no lines etched into his dark brown skin. His lips were smooth. And his chin line was sharp, reminding her of the sharp angles she so loved in the facial structures of her sons. His hair was characteristically matted, long and tangled into sections which must once have been braids. As soon as she looked up at him he opened his coat, pulling apart layers of clothing like a thick curtain, baring a thin, beautiful chest which was covered sparsely with tiny black curls. Quickly, she returned her eyes to her lap and shifted away from him in her seat. He remained, however, despite her discomfort; because of it, perhaps. He stood before her, holding his layers of shirts and sweaters opened, exposing his naked chest, as if it were a work of art containing some hidden message she was expected to see. As soon as the train pulled into her station, she rushed out the door. She breathed deeply, closed her eyes to regain her composure.

So intensely were Julia's thoughts focussed on these things—the South African poet, the crying, the handsome man smiling at her, the homeless man with the bared chest—that she crossed the street against the light and was startled into ordinary consciousness by the loud honking of a horn. Why had all these things happened in one day? Or did they happen every day, the only thing which made them special this day being the quality of her noticing? Someone jerked her across the street. "Watch where you're going honey," he said. Julia leaned against a mailbox and adjusted her coat. She forced herself to pay attention to the street as she headed for the fruit and vegetable stand at the end of the block where she would buy fresh broccoli and the large blueberry muffins Anthony and Daniel liked so much.

For weeks, Anthony had been angry at her, an anger which she knew from her experience with Daniel, would be chronic and periodic for years to come. But Daniel and Julia had been angry at each other periodically ever since he was two. Her older son was so much like her, Julia felt, he had to extend his anger between them, a heavy tool inserted in a small crack to break a lock. When his anger escalated during the early years of adolescence Julia was used to it. It was only a difference in degree. "I get angry at you but I love you very much," she and Daniel had been assuring each other for as long as she could remember.

But Anthony's love had never been forced by strong ambivalence into the security of flexibility. Until recently, he still curled up next to her each evening, a physical requirement before he could sleep. He stroked her hair, told her she was beautiful. Sometimes he wrote poems which he showed her in secret. But she had encouraged him to take pride in the short emotional explosions he scratched on pads and napkins. She typed them, showing him how they achieved a new meaning when placed carefully on a page. She bought him a white notebook in which to file the poems and wrote his name on the cover. Then suddenly he stopped embracing her. His kisses were perfunctory. He fought with her over the details of housekeeping chores, over the need for a hat in the rain. For weeks she said nothing, knowing she must let him do this, feeling like a lover who knows a passionate affair is about to end and watches with a strange distance which is sacrifice, resignation and protection all at once. Years ago, Julia would have been ashamed to speak, even to herself, of the passion she felt for her sons, the way in which language, when she spoke of them, reflected the emotions of erotic love. But shame was no longer equal to the task of covering this truth: the children had changed her life. By the very purity of their dependence on her, they had demanded everything she could give, which was often insufficient. And between the two—the giving and the insufficiency—she had been tied to them for years by her deepest attention. And attention—the willingness to look continually, to not turn away, to move around contours, touching, standing back, trying to comprehend the singular meaning of a line, a word, another mind (all were equally mysterious to her, equally compelling)—that *regard*, or attention, was all she knew of any kind of love. "Want to come shopping with me?" she'd asked Anthony, trying to entice him into one of their old favorite activities. They would walk down Broadway together, stopping haphazardly in various stores, holding hands, talking about all the things that cluttered their equally active minds. But he had refused. "I don't mean to hurt your feelings Mom. But it's kind of boring," he said, and turned away.

She had never actually said to herself: I will not cry again, after all those years during which she had cried so often and intensely she had decided it was remarkable that tears were never used up, produced in an infinite supply until death, like waste products, or blood. Often she wished she could cry but succeeded only in making short, high pitched sounds, like a wounded dog. Hearing the dog sounds, Bruce would think she was crying. He would run his fingers across her cheeks, hoping for tears. But she would be dry-eyed, and they would turn onto their backs, stare at the ceiling, both of them oddly disappointed. She had learned to be satisfied with heat as a biological reaction to pain. Heat rushed through her body while a cold sweat broke out on her face and neck. "Are you upset?" Bruce would ask sometimes, when he knew she was thinking about how she used to write, or after she'd had a fight with one of the boys or with him. And she got used to answering, he to hearing—"No, I'm just hot."

Julia waited as the cashier weighed the broccoli and tomatoes, rang up soy sauce, muffins, white squares of tofu floating like unnaturally geometrical fish entrapped in the cloudy water of the plastic bag.

She *would* watch the news with Anthony and Daniel, she decided as she shifted the groceries to one arm and rang for the elevator. Anthony might be upset, but he had to be hardened, encouraged to become more like his father. She could become furious at Bruce for his capacity to endure disaster—as if he expected nothing from the world but injustice and disappointment. "That's not it at all," he would tell her. "I know there's injustice. But there's happiness too. You're the one who only sees the suffering," he accused. She hoped he would come home early enough to watch the news with them, help her explain things to Anthony. She worried about him, still so raw to every feeling, suffering stomach aches, insomnia, what he called his "bad feelings" at every small experience of pain.

When Daniel was younger he too had refused to watch films which depicted suffering, especially stories about American slavery. He couldn't bear the thought of people's misery, he said, couldn't stand the thought of a beating or a lynching. But now, at sixteen, he criticized his brother for over-sensitivity. "Just do what I do," Daniel instructed when Anthony wept at the state of the homeless in New York, the killing of Martin Luther King which he studied in school, the kidnapped children whose faces stared out from the sides of milk cartons at the breakfast table. "I just watch it," Daniel said, "and I say to myself—I am here. Sitting in my chair. I'm not that person on the screen. You can watch the most violent movies if you learn to do it right. I can watch the absolutely most violent movies in the world and not get scared. I just keep telling myself—it's not me. It's only actors up there."

"That's movies, Daniel. I'm not talking about movies."

"The homeless aren't actors, Daniel," Julia chided, instantly regretting her words. What Daniel hated most about her, he said, was her endless moralism.

"I know Mom," he said, anger already lacing his voice. "But still. It's the principle of the thing."

After she unpacked the groceries and changed her clothes, Julia told the boys about the South African poet and that she wanted them to watch the news with her. Anthony looked nervous. "I don't know if I can take it," he said.

"Try," Julia insisted. "We have to know about these things. They aren't going to show him getting killed on TV, Anthony. We have to pay attention."

"I don't even want to think about it," said Anthony.

"I agree with Mom, it's important to know what's going on in the world," said Daniel, and he plopped into a large chair close to the TV. Julia, always grateful for her older son's rare support, kissed his forehead as she walked by him to sit near Anthony. "Maybe there'll be a reprieve," she said, taking her son's hand.

But when Dan Rather had finished the top story—about a hospital in the West Indies which claimed to have a cure for AIDS—and the South African poet's face appeared on the screen, Bruce walked in and said, "He's dead. They killed him today."

There were shots of the prison near Capetown, high imposing walls of ancient stone. The poet's mother, a small bent woman cloaked in black, walked quickly past the camera. One of her supporters motioned impatiently with his hand: *leave her alone.*

"I can't stand it." Anthony bolted from the room.

"Oh God," Daniel sighed, impatiently.

And now Julia found herself defending her younger son. "It is terribly painful, and he's very sensitive, Daniel," she said. She coughed, rubbed her eyes. Bruce looked at her—interested—and took a long sip of his wine.

Anthony had remained in the hallway, anxiously eyeing the television during a commercial. "Then why'd you make me watch," he accused her. "I told you I'd be petrified."

They all turned back to the television screen, Daniel and Julia sitting in the living room, Bruce glancing up intermittently as he fixed his dinner, Anthony from the hallway, peeking out then jumping back behind the wall. The poet's face, an old black and white photograph, covered the screen again, and she could see the lines on his cheeks were the ritual scars received in puberty. Then the photograph was replaced by film of mourners surrounding the poet's mother, his wife, his children. Bishop Tutu was speaking to a crowd of demonstrators. "They killed a poet today," he said.

"I told you I couldn't stand this," Anthony screamed. "Why'd you make me watch this Mommy! It's all your fault!" He came back into the living room and sat close to his father who was eating his dinner while sitting on the couch.

"It's not you getting killed. I keep telling you, just remember that and you can take anything," Daniel repeated, grabbing an orange juice carton and taking a long gulp.

"Don't drink from the quart," said Julia, trying to change the subject and ward off a fight. But Anthony screamed at his brother, "Well I just can't do it. I'm not like you, okay?"

"You've got to learn. How're you gonna get along in this world?" said Daniel, a deep-voiced echo of Julia's words.

"Maybe those feelings of Anthony's are important to hang onto," said Bruce.

"Dad!" Daniel shouted, his shoulders hunched forward slightly, his neck stiff with rage at this betrayal. "What do you do? Cry every time there's some injustice in the world?"

"No," Bruce admitted. "But maybe I wish I did."

Anthony smirked through his tears. Daniel walked angrily into his room where, he once confessed to Julia, he often cried as much as Anthony did, but privately.

Late that night Anthony called Julia into his room. He was unable to sleep, so filled was he with the bad feeling. She sat on his bed and listened to him cry.

"I know I've been mean to you," he said. "And I don't know why."

Julia forced herself to explain to Anthony that it was natural, he was growing up, pulling away from her.

"I don't want to pull away from you," he wept. "I don't want to grow up,"—which alarmed Julia, so she whispered to him about how all children had to grow up and become independent of their parents, but she would always be his mother, he would always be her child. She assured him he wouldn't grow up until he was ready, that it was a slow process, just the beginning. That it was exciting, necessary, full of pleasures he could not yet imagine.

A few weeks before, as they lounged around the livingroom on a Sunday afternoon, Daniel had asked whose hand was bigger now, Anthony's or Julia's. Julia held up her hand, fingers stretched to measure, but Anthony had hidden his behind his back, saying, "I don't want to know." "Growing up is a good thing," she had told him then. "You can write a poem about it." "*You* don't write anymore," Anthony said.

Now she held his lanky torso across her lap and fingered his thick curls. Soon he quieted down. "I'm scared," he said. She caressed his head, his face. "I won't let anything bad happen to you," she told him automatically. But she knew he was thinking about the poet. "I'll always love you best," he whispered in a small boy's voice. Julia rocked him, knowing he was falling asleep, but she heard the words resonating like a fading echo. She slid him off her lap and tucked him in. She was about to leave the room but suddenly she was sitting on the floor, her face buried in his quilt, raw with the loss she knew was inevitable and necessary, the loss from which she felt she might never recover and which she nevertheless had to encourage, even insist upon. She berated herself for self-pity. Was her son in prison? Was he dead? She touched Anthony's fingers, now soft with sleep. Still, she kept hearing the echo—I'll always love you best; if it were true, she was frightened, if false, bereft.

She went over to Daniel's bed where he breathed the rhythmical breaths of the deepest level of sleep, and she sat beside this son whose leaving had been taking place since the day he learned to walk. She felt proud of Daniel's fierce boundaries, for his determination to be different from her. She felt grateful that Daniel had never made her cry with his pubescent rages because he had made it clear for so long that his passion was not her, but the world.

That night, in her deep sleep, Julia felt her life threatened. She tried to awaken, part of her knowing she was dreaming and in the dream was in danger of being killed, part of her still in the dream, succumbing to the imminent attack. She felt Bruce shake her and call her name.

"You're dreaming, honey. You're dreaming."

Finally, she pulled herself out of the dream, into the dark, cool room she had shared with Bruce for twenty years. The beige cotton curtains ballooned with air and then pasted again to the glass. The soothing greens, browns and whites of the room looked deep grey in the semi-dark. She covered her face with her hands. "I was being killed," she said. As soon as she said it she remembered–she was not being killed. Someone was taking Daniel from her. It was Daniel who was in danger. He was being dragged or pushed or sucked away, and from the look on his face he had no idea of the danger he was in. Julia had screamed in her dream as Daniel disappeared.

"In two years he'll be going to college," she whispered to Bruce.

"Who? Daniel? I know. Was that your dream?" His voice cracked slightly with emotion reflecting hers. She turned her back to him but lay very close so that her shoulders and buttocks touched his chest and thighs. He held her and began to lift his hands to her breasts, but she moved away from him.

"I'm sorry," he said.

Then the amnesia broke. She had forgotten the *desire* to be open. Once it had not been a fear, but a yearning.

She almost turned around in the comforting dark of the familiar room, the bed in which her children had been conceived, where she and Bruce had made love hundreds of times, felt themselves to be almost one person, and then more different from each other than from anyone else in the world. She felt lost to him in the cloudy dark, unseen; unseen. She could begin a story with this feeling, she thought—with the African poet, the crying, the bare chest of the homeless man. Like the world pulled Daniel something outside herself was pulling her. But she only raised Bruce's fingers to her lips.

"No, I'm the one who's sorry," she said. "I'm too upset, that's all."

Long ago she would have sunk into sex as a comfort, wanting the moment when she would feel unprotected, completely light, and free. Weeks, even a few days before, she would have felt only heat—that strange, enveloping fever she'd grown used to as a sign that she might be in pain. Now she felt cold, shaken with chills as if she were the young man with the bare chest. She had looked away, but now she rose from her subway seat and held him. He lay his head on her shoulder and she felt the stressed and tightened muscles in his back. He leaned heavily against her, but she could not remain aloof, and she touched his hair, ran her finger down the swollen vein in his temple, his angular jaw which reminded her of Daniel, of Anthony.

Water Skiing

Harriet Malinowitz

I. During, Looking at After

It's going to end. I know it, even though we are lying face to face on Jellis' bed, smiling at each other. She was about to walk out the door to go to work when I called her back.

"Come back a minute," I said, in the tone of an imperious, illogical child. She looked humorously put upon, exactly the response I expected, and she climbed back into bed, pretending to be pretending reluctance.

"What?" she says.

I put my arms around her. "You thrill me," I say. I want to say something a little more comfortably beside the point, but she has been thrilling me excruciatingly all weekend and I am bursting to say so; and because she does not see herself as thrilling, I know she could do with hearing it.

There is an increased pressure of her arms around me. "Get some more sleep," she whispers. We hug firmly; then she gets up, we wave, she walks out the door. Again, her whole body implies wry reluctance. I wonder if it is true, or if she is relieved to walk out the door and feel the cloak of solitude wrap around her again. I lie in her bed, stroking her cat, soaking in the nuances of the silent apartment that is hers, where I am now alone. This is the most purely I ever have her, in these minutes between the time she leaves for work and when I leave, when I turn my head on her pillows, which are made of a different texture and density than my pillows, and I look at her phone which is unplugged (as mine never is), and the stark expanses of floor and wall that she calls "the ascetic mode." On a table at the bedside is a pad of canary memo paper with her name logoed across the bottom, the only visible sign of frivolity, of self-attention, in the room. This room is her, to be digested whole in a way that she, the person, never can be. The person only offers pieces of herself in measured doses. I accept them cautiously, like a drug I will like too much and must be careful not to get addicted to.

I have a key to this apartment. I can let myself in and out and lock the door behind me. She trusts me not to read anything I shouldn't. Someday I will not have this kind of access. I don't think she will ever ask me to return my key; but one day I will take it off my ring and put it in a box, and when I come to visit I'll buzz the downstairs buzzer, knock on her door, and wait to be allowed in. There are always limits and rules, but right now some of them are suspended. Sometimes these days I have the key to her face; she trusts me to read what I see there. Sometimes when I am inside her face I can't believe that what I see there could ever change; but in my saner moments I can't believe that it won't. Human beings enter other human beings like tape cassettes: you put them in, you play them, and then they are ejected.

I get up, dress, prepare to leave. The cat runs around my feet. I wonder who she thinks I am, whether she believes I belong here. As I close the door behind me I photograph the room with my eyes. There is really no need to do that now, this is just an ordinary day among others. I will go to work, about 11:00 I will call her at her office, and tonight or maybe tomorrow night I will be back. If I spend a night alone it won't be a tragedy, I'll enjoy stretching my body to the four corners of my double bed. It will only be a hiatus of calm before we re-converge. This room is part of the scenario of my current life; I should indulge in the luxury of taking it for granted. But my pupils widen as they see it for one last moment, they cling to it until the closed door blots it out.

The weekend that just ended: Friday night. Jellis calls me after work. She wants to come over before some others do so we can squeeze in a little time alone. I rush to accomplish the few tasks I have, feeling the thrill of conspiracy, that we are each compelled by the same sneaky motive of clandestinely absorbing some of the other. But it doesn't work. My friend Nancy rings the bell first. A little later Jellis comes in, expecting to find me alone. Her face never loses its friendly smile; no one but I would ever know what other expression might have been there in its place. She is the first WASP I have ever been intimately acquainted with, and the cryptic outer manifestations of her feelings baffle, frustrate, and scare me in their deft avoidance of candor. She has told me that my voice, walk, posture are completely readable, that my body cannot tell a lie. For me, it is part of her amazing complexity that she can manage to appear so nondescript.

She goes to the refrigerator and takes a beer to the sofa. She always sits tentatively, never as if she plans to stay for very long, never as if she feels she belongs anywhere. She is wearing a white tailored shirt with the sleeves rolled up, and jeans. Her blond hair falls in her face; periodically she brushes it back, out of the path of her beer can. There are very few material objects that she seems to associate with comfortably, but with beer cans and tailored shirts she always appears at home; they are her province.

I move around the room, putting things away. I talk to both of them, ostensibly at the same time, but I am forced to alternate: I say one thing the way I talk to Nancy, one thing the way I talk to Jellis. I have to prove to Jellis that I wish we were alone, that even in the presence of others there's a private circuit between us which remains unbroken. I have to prove to Nancy that I'm not coupled beyond recognition, that ours is an old friendship that predates my relationship with Jellis and we still share a primary intimacy. Jellis will leave; Nancy will stay; I feel this intuitively. Nancy and I are like the Grand Canyon, something that will forever deepen and magnificently weather millenia of erosion. Jellis and I are like Mt. Vesuvius—a supreme explosion at a specific point in time. After the explosion there will be lots of devastating ash and hot molten lava; but finally the lava and ash will settle, and the damage they have done will recede in memory. The visible signs will disappear, and only perhaps some permanent climatic change, difficult to connect with the original eruption, will remain.

More people come in. They are my friends, they have

been forced on Jellis. Again, I hover between showing that my allegiance to them is unbroken, and assuring Jellis that I am her port in this unsolicited social storm. Inevitably, I move to Jellis. Every look or wink or smile that passes between us further crystallizes our intimacy and drives another wedge between my friends and me. I am walking further and further out on a precipice, placing all my faith in some lovely net below which is spread out tantalizingly but has not promised to catch me. Every time I look at Jellis and she looks at me our circuit hums with voltage, the current runs swiftly. I can't resist doing this, again and again.

My friends are tolerating me for now, but later on they'll make me atone for my defection. I've always been a militant champion of singlehood; now all of a sudden I've gone off the deep end, have started acting like one of those couply clones I used to make fun of. What makes them somewhat more benevolent in dealing with me is their belief, like mine, that this can't continue, at least not at this level. I'm going through a tumultuous phase, like adolescence; when the honeymoon is over I will once again be fully accountable for my actions. They believe this, I believe it—and Jellis?

One day several months ago, in the spring, we met for lunch in Central Park. We had been together about four months. We sat on a bench facing a pond and talked about that all-consuming topic: ourselves. Two people sitting side by side on a park bench, trying to describe their feelings for each other, not sure what kind of dose to measure out—afraid that the truth would be too large, tempted to pour out only a little, but driven by the need for honesty and relief to be precise.

That was when I said that I felt the way I did the one

time in my life I tried to water ski. At first, every time the boat took off with me behind it, I fell right over. This was frustrating and disappointing, but at least it wasn't scary—it was a simple plop in the water. Over and over again I tried to get up and stay up, and finally I did. Suddenly, without warning, I was upright and careening around the lake at a terrifying speed. The world whizzed by as one enormous, overpowering vibration. I was where I'd struggled to be—but all I could think was—Oh God, how am I going to get out of this one alive?

"That's just how I feel," said Jellis.

As time goes by, it only gets worse. Now it's the summer, and we're still zooming madly around the lake, but I know that eventually we'll have to stop, we'll get tired, our bodies will give out, the boat will run out of gas—and when we feel that slack on the rope we'll fall with a terrible crash. That's how things have to happen in life—everything ends. And we know it, there's always, in everything, this death-in-life; you can see the extinguishing instrument if you look hard enough into the flame.

II. After, Looking at During

When the worst has happened, you go on with life. First there are weeks when you feel like a mass of torn cartilege, or like a house is sitting on your head, squashing you down to one dimension—or it seems that something is rumbling at the core of you, trying to push out in every direction, ready to explode out of every hole and pore. This is the violent time.

Then there's the quiet, the waking up to a life that's pale, not colored, to rhythmic, steady breathing that doesn't falter. You move through streets, get on and off trains, feel the getting out of bed in the morning and getting into it at night as parts of a swift, unrelenting cycle which catches you in its centrifugal force.

The end comes like a déjà vu: it has been lived so many times already. We thrash out the pain between us for a while, and then we stop speaking to each other. It's like a death, only not like it, because you can't yearn with any hope for life after death when you are both still alive but not doing anything about it.

In a friend's house I find a magazine with pictures of John Lennon and Yoko Ono. I take it home and I stare at them for hours. Yoko wears clothes and gazes out impassively, while naked John clings to her like a baby monkey who for the first time has been given something other than a wire surrogate mother. In other pictures they appear to be welded side by side, like Siamese twins. I go to see a play about John Lennon. In one part John and Yoko go to Janov, the "primal scream" therapist, for therapy. They are put in separate rooms, each suffering, the severed halves each straining toward the other, like amputees trying to reconnect with what's been cut to stop the phantom pain.

I attend a crowded conference in a large hotel in our big city. Across the room, Jellis comes into my field of vision. She's wearing a loose red shirt I've never seen before. I feel stabbed, betrayed: she has a new shirt. Her cells have started to reproduce and die, she's not the same person she was before, she's changed. The noise of the many women at the conference, in that room, is like the muted background music of an old movie. Nonsensically, but making perfect sense for the first time, the words of that song float through my head: "You will see a stranger across a crowded room." My grandfather, a great romantic, used to sing this at the kitchen table, and now I hear resonating in my head the baritone of this ancestor of mine who stayed married for fifty years and had four children and eight grandchildren: "You will see a stranger across a crowded room." My grandfather and the other romantics of that age believed that this song was about a beginning, that this stranger was someone to whom in time you would grow inexorably welded. He never prepared me for this—that it could all happen in reverse, that after incredible intimacy you could see someone across a crowded room, and she is a stranger.

And yet, I think fiercely, I know that after this she will go to work, because it's Thursday and she works the night shift on Thursday. She'll work until 11:00, and then she'll go home. I know how she'll walk up the steps in front of her building, and how the downstairs hall will smell, and what sound will echo from the hollow stairs as she walks the flight to her apartment, and exactly what pressure of the key will be required as she turns it in the lock, and how her cat will run to meet her when she enters the dark apartment, and how she'll turn on the overhead light and talk to her. I know just how she'll run the bath, and take off her clothes, and what the bathtub will feel like, and the soap will smell like, and what her body will look like and feel like and smell like; and I know just how hard the bed will be when she lies down on it, and how the texture of the blankets will be, and precisely what the dent in the pillows will be.

I own part of her forever, because I studied so hard, I sucked and breathed in her details until they were swimming in my bloodstream.

At least, I own part of her forever until she changes her details. And she's already changed her shirt.

Is the glass of water half empty or half full? When we were together I clung to the good things and blocked out the bad things; now I cling to the bad things and block out the good things.

The good things can eat me; but it is, in fact, a relief to finally admit the bad things that I used to keep drugged and speechless. To finally look through the holes in the Wonder Bread and see clearly that it had never made anyone's body grow strong in twelve ways. To finally admit that Jellis was like a beautiful notebook whose pages were all stuck together. To finally say callously of my sacred love: "What a stiff!"

This is the memory of her I cherish most: one day last summer, we went to the beach. Hot air reached through the open car windows as we crawled along the Southern State Parkway in Saturday traffic. Our conversation was sluggish. I usually made most of it, but my battery was running low just then. I wished we had something exciting to say to each other. When we got to the beach we plopped down on our towels on the sand. We lay back, our faces to the sun. Jellis said:

"So, tell me what you think about..."

My heart thudded with an anticipatory thrill. She was finally going to introduce something juicy.

"...my new file cabinet."

I felt totally deflated. And outraged that she didn't wonder anything more complex about my thoughts. I didn't show it, though. I said, "I like it. It's nice." She was satisfied. Everything she wanted to know was answered.

Can you see why this is my most cherished memory of

Jellis Jones, my true love? I cling to it like a woman holding onto the ledge of a building out of whose window she has just been pushed.

There are other things I remember, too, scenes that play themselves out in succession in my head like a long ballad in which the lyrics change from stanza to stanza but the tune remains maddeningly the same. The times she got sick and banned me from her apartment, insisting on being left alone—only to explode later that I had abandoned her, I should have known that she wanted me there but couldn't say so. The times she'd slip an extra pillow behind my back while we sat talking on her bed, or dig my car out when the snow plow buried it, or remember to take the things I'd need on a weekend out of the city that she knew I'd forget—the little protective gestures that at first made my chest contract painfully—and then the times that she seemed to vanish into some cold, dark tunnel, and a mechanically smiling facsimile of her would appear in her place, offering the same beneficient gestures which I didn't want to accept and lacked the words to refuse. Even after we were finished, her helpful gestures continued to appear like smiling plastic dolls tirelessly popping off an assembly line.

"No, thank you," I finally said one day when I ran into her on the street. I had just emerged from a laundromat carrying a huge stuffed laundry bag, which she had tried to take from me. "When I need services, I'll call the Salvation Army."

And yet how addicted I'd gotten to those services, to that delicious cushion that padded the hard edges of aloneness and self-reliance. Sometimes I felt like Frankenstein's monster, an invention of someone else's imagination—a singular species thrust into a strange new world it had been given no reasonable chance to adapt to. I'd always carried my own laundry before, but it seemed that Jellis had tricked those muscles into atrophying, lulling them to sleep with love and then dropping an extra heavy load on them before they'd had a chance to awaken and flex.

After we broke up she said it was like drowning, every hurtful thing I had ever done flashed before her eyes.

I could tell you my side of it. I could try to tell you her side of it. I could tell it with anger, or with sorrow, or I could tell it with the feeling I sometimes have of carrying a dead fetus around in my stomach. I could tell it analytically, or comically, romantically or tragically. I could explain a little better who she is—or was—and who I am and who I was, so that we would emerge as two distinct people with our own unique "issues."

But what's the point. It's over—and it will be over for centuries—forever, until the end of time, which is a meaningless expression because time will never end, it will go on long after this collusion among living beings on this earth has ended. It was something that happened once, and its overness is the real and lasting part ever so much more than its itness. Its moment of being over was like a death sentence on the love—from that moment on the love started to self-destruct, because if it didn't, we would, and the whole crazy process of falling in love and growing in love was turned on its head and went into reverse.

I always used to say that breaking up is like trying to go down a road in two different directions at the same time. You walk away from the wreck, determinedly striding from where you've lodged for so long to some new, unknown destination. And yet at the same time you can't help wanting to march right back to where you came from, to that place that's so familiar and that you've come to call home. You keep getting sucked back because it seems that maybe, maybe it's still there; maybe it didn't get wracked by Cossacks after all; maybe there's still some soup simmering unattended on the stove.

But finally, there's proof: a peek sneaked at dusk through the hedges reveals only a shell, charred ash, and it's possible, once and for all, to walk down the road with singleminded purpose and know that there's nothing left to get homesick for.

It's many months later now; after stomping back and forth over that road so many times that I practically wore through the pavement, I packed my bags and left for good. I don't even like Jellis anymore. I was madly in love with her—consummately, where I felt pieces of her floated in every cell of my body—and now I'm detoxified, out of love with her.

It's so hard to love somebody. I know that there are people who fall in and out of relationships with relative grace and ease, as if dancing to the patented choreography of a nationally syndicated dance studio. But I can't understand it. It seems to me that you must spend an inordinate amount of time trying to find someone whose loveableness strikes you in your gut, whose essence satisfies your own freak craving. And yet, as the analytical politicos say, here is the primary contradiction: that once you've found that person, there inevitably comes a time when you have to annul that love, to eradicate it, to reassess that rare coin so that you can pronounce it counterfeit, common, without value. This, too, is considered a great achievement. Sometimes it's a toss-up as to which takes more energy: to create or to destroy.

Years ago, in a college freshman philosophy class, they taught us this paradox: you can never get from here to there. The reason is that between any two points there is a midpoint, and when you reach that midpoint it becomes a starting point from which you reach another midpoint—and it continues, ad infinitum. So, the theory goes, you will endlessly arrive at midpoint after midpoint; it is in principle impossible to arrive at the end of the road.

And that, I think, is why relationships are beyond being figured out. They don't start the first time you sleep together, or at the first acknowledgement of feeling, or even when you meet each other; they start way back at the moment you are conceived, or perhaps when some trauma inflicted outside the womb causes a ripple in the amniotic fluid, and the seeds of some future disturbance, twenty or thirty or forty years in the future, are planted. The fears, the anger, the needs begin to take shape, and years later two of these former embrionic dots meet, the accrued experiences of their lives stored like a vast accumulation of data that can be called up at any time on a video screen. The ways they will meet, the ways they will clash, the ways they will miss each other are all coded and quietly waiting. They see each other for the first time and think that this is the beginning, but it's not—anymore than the end is the end. You think you will go somewhere together; later on you look back and try to figure out where you've gone; but all there is is an endless procession of midpoints, times when you were becoming, aging, when you were on the way.

One day more than two years ago, Jellis and I broke up for a weekend, and then we got back together. The next morning she went to work and I had a Sealy Posturepedic mattress delivered. She decided to leave work at 10 a.m. to come over and try out the Sealy. It rained outside all day and I felt happier than I could remember ever feeling before. I thought that life would be different now; we had cured each other's loneliness and sorrow. I couldn't wait to race off into the future with her, but we never met quite so perfectly again. I thought it was a step up the ladder of joy, but it turned out to be the top rung; by the time we realized it, we were climbing down the other side.

Mamie

Carolina Mancuso

So I says to 'im, that's it, I says, I'm a person too, I won't take no more. Get out, I says. Can't do nothin' right for you no more, better if ya leave. You made yer choice, now I got to make mine. That's it now, that's it.

I was straight with him. An' calm. So calm I didn't know myself. All the while I'm thinkin', who's talkin', who's sayin' those words I hear?

Not that I ever yelled much. There was that time with Jake down at the corner store, he says Mitzie lifted a bar a soap. Not five she was, quiet as a mouse, wouldn't touch a crumb ya didn't put right in her hand. Go ahead, I says, puttin' my eyes through Jake like kitchen knives. Go ahead, look in her coat if ya got to. Ya can look in mine too, ya ole vulture, ya know damn well you won't find no soap. Ain't no more soap in that child's hands than those onions weighed a pound without yer fat thumb on 'em. Folks starvin' in the streets, an' you soakin' 'em fer every last penny, an' then some.

Withered up like a dyin' vine, Jake did. Effie his wife, she come outside an' put 'n arm around me, whisperin'—though he couldn'ta heard a word. Ya done right, she says, old coot needs a hundred times that. She gimme a hug an' all of a sudden, whaddaya know but we're both cryin', an' then she just slips away.

Ain't like it didn't cost me nothin', ya know, takin' a stand against that so-and-so. Always hurt me more to yell than anybody listenin'. But when it needs doin', I guess I'm as good as the next one.

Not a month went by, ya know, Jake died in his sleep. Blood-poison. Guess his own body couldn't stand 'im. Nobody cried a drop, not even Effie, leastwise she never cried fer him. But that Bea, ya know, she comes to tell me an' whaddaya think she says? She says, Mamie, it's you, ya done it with yer eyes.

That's Bea for ya, what a scorcher. Bea's my ladyfriend upstairs. We been friends a long time now. Let's see, Sammy an' me, we moved in here, come January, it'll be thirty-six years. Bea an' me been friends now just about as long as Sammy an' me was married. She knows me pretty good by now. She can tell ya I ain't the yellin' type. She says I'm too kind, I let people step on me. Then she says, but ya know, Mamie, you got somethin' else goin' for ya, she says. You got those godawful, steam-rollin', fire-bubblin' eyes. An' you know how to use 'em, she says. Then she shakes her head, givin' me a look like she's so scairt. Gits me laughin' every time. Blushin' like a kid. Oh, I ain't much fer boastin', never was. But I know what I got that's good. An' it's true, them eyes a broke through stone, if ya know what I mean. Fancy, Sammy use to say it was the fire in my eyes that brought 'im to me. An' there's Bea sayin' it was the ice that drove 'im away. She says I done that too with my eyes.

One time Bea an' me had a fight, an' she called 'em devil eyes, evil eyes, like Italian folks says. Can't think what we was fightin' over. Spent a whole night settin' up talkin, Sammy an' Tom an' the kids all sound asleep. The sun comes up, grinnin' in the kitchen window, an' there's Bea an' me, still sittin' at the table, cryin' an' sighin', an' yackin' away, talkin' 'bout the times way before we knew each other, 'bout when we was kids.

Then Bea says to me, oh, Mamie, the *sadness* in them eyes. She says, why, if the body that owns them eyes is still alive, then even *I* got hope. Then she hugs me, her voice hushed-up like in church, an' all of a sudden it's like Mamma huggin' me again, like Mamma standin' over me washin' out the cuts Johnny gimme with the glass he smashed at the kitchen wall. Mamma's voice cooin' at me, but mad too, shakin' an' hushed up so the neighbors don't hear no more. Like a hand strokin' at my brow, that voice, sayin' it ain't natural, honey, what you come to expect, a brother rippin' at yer face. I know it makes ya mad enough to wish to kill, an' by God, honey, Mamma says, you got a right, you got a right....

That day, ya know, he come home rantin' again, Sammy did. Like a madman. All juiced up. Come at me like an axe to a dry woodpile. Never laid a hand on me, that man. Big point a pride with him. Never laid a hand on my woman, he says. Stone me with words, though, hailstones smashin' me to bits til I was crawlin' across the ground. Ain't had no schoolin' to speak of, but born with words on his tongue, that man. Coulda been a lawyer, I use to say, judge and jury woulda scream for mercy. Sammy aims his words like guns fer the soft spots, an' he don't miss. Every damn time I end up thinkin' it's me, I musta done wrong again. No woman a mine, he says. No woman a mine! Like he owns a piece a my head! But you mark me now, what he done with words, I done just as good with looks.

So he come home late that day, rantin' again, late for supper. What supper if he don't bring no food? Got a couple hours work haulin' boxes, left all smiles in the mornin'. Turns up late, juiced up an' no food nor money. I ask him where the food money's gone, smellin' where it went, his hot wind in my face. An' all of a sudden, he just comes apart like a glued-up cup in my hand. Starts a-wailin'.

It fell through, Mamie, he says. It was just fer today. Ain't got no job, Mamie, he says.

As if I don't know. What in the hell made him figure two hours work was a whole damn job? Ain't he seen enough a these times yet? This man's feet ain't nowhere near the ground.

Ain't got no job, Mamie, he goes on. What am I gonna do? Ain't no work nowhere.

I put my arms 'round him, he's slobberin' on my shoulder. Now don't get me wrong, I don't mind a man cryin'. I always says if they done it more, like we do, they'd be better off. Awful lotta strength comes from wipin' tears, ya know, yer own an' everybody else's. Not that I don't wish there was another way. But ya know, it was only bein' so juiced up that made 'im cry. And that don't count, if ya know what I mean. That's only slobberin', it ain't the real thing.

So I hold him an' talk soft, sayin' it ain't his fault, ain't everybody we know in the same boat. Lookit Harry Weinman, with that big job in the mill, struttin' around playin' foreman, don't he git cut out one of the first? Lookit Bernie, he ain't had no work for a whole year now. An' Bea, she's goin' nuts with Tom, he don't even wanna get outta bed. It's the times, I tell him, it ain't you. (Meanwhile I'm thinkin', how many times have I gotta tell him?) Maybe Bill was right, I say. Maybe we gotta do somethin' together.

Now what made me bring up Bill while he's slobberin' on me, I just don't know. Sometimes things stick in my head an' I can't let go of 'em, but what in the hell made me talk about Bill?

See, Bill an' Emily come over one night the week before. Bill's all hepped up, sayin' how people gonna go out marchin' in the streets, try an' get things changed, try an' get themselves heard. Make the gover'ment see how hard it is for us folks. It's wrong, he says, livin' this way. But we can change it, he says, if we do it together.

Sammy looks at him like he's got two heads. Yer crazy, he yells, you got rocks in yer skull. Gover'ment's doin' all it can. Ain't we got the best in FDR? If things can change, he'll do it. He's the only one can make 'em change.

But Bill goes on 'bout jobs for everybody that needs 'em. Shorter hours, better pay. An' even money to pay folks that don't have no work. He says how the money's out there, stuffin' up rich folks' pockets. An' the more he talks, the more I like what he says, til my heart starts to pound just thinkin' 'bout it.

Maybe he's got somethin', I says to Sammy. It's true what he says, things ought not to be this way. Then I turn to Bill. Well, maybe I'll go with ya one of these days, I says. Women can come, can't they? Then Emily says, why sure they can come, Mamie. I'm goin', women can do it, too.

You come along with us, Mamie.

Emily an' I sit there grinnin', thinkin' 'bout women marchin' in the street, til there's Sammy bouncin' his head up 'an down between us, mockin' the way we look. For the resta the night, that old fool fussed an' fumed an' mocked everythin' we said. Finally, Bill an' Emily excuse themselves that they gotta go, givin' me looks like they sure are sorry, an' am I gonna be all right? Don't you worry, I tell 'em with my eyes, I ain't scared a this old coot.

Well, no sooner the door shuts than Sammy's at me like a mad dog. I seen it comin' that time, so I just set down with my coffee an' watch it, like I was watchin' the sun set on a lazy day. But that's when I started seein' it all clear, how nuts he went since he lost his job. Crossin' the street to keep from meetin' somebody he knew, yellin' an' screamin' if I wanted us to go visitin' or take a little walk outside. Turned sour like a rotten peach, turned bad on people, like he could live without 'em. Turned bad on me.

I just don't git it even now. Me, the worse things git, the more I need folks near me. But not Sammy. Pushes people away, an' cuts 'em up like he has to show they ain't perfect neither. Most of the time he's yellin' 'bout anythin' but what's really goin' on.

That night he went on fer hours. 'Bout Bill an' Emily, 'bout FDR, 'bout my family, don't ask me where they come in, 'bout me, what a bad woman I am, even *thinkin'* 'bout goin' out marchin' in the street. No woman a mine, he says over an' over, like I'm his old beagle dog.

Finally, he sits down, with that look on his face like him bein' the man, he's got to save me from somethin' I can't figure out on my own, like he come to his senses that he was drainin' his lungs at somebody too dumb to git it. So he looks at me real calm, like at a kid.

Stay away from 'em, he says. They're commies.

What? I ask him. Who?

Bill an' Emily. They're commies. They're against everythin' that's the way things oughta be. They're bad. They wanna see the whole United States gover'ment go up in smoke. They wanna take over the world.

I shake my head, tryin' to picture Bill an' Emily burnin' up Washington, D.C.

Dontcha see, he says, they wanna take away yer money an' give it to everybody else.

Sammy, we ain't got no money, I says.

Well, after that, you can see why bringin' up Bill an' Emily while Sammy's slobberin' on my shoulder might not a been the best thing I coulda done. But ain't he slobberin' 'bout not havin' a job, an' ain't Bill an' Emily talkin' 'bout how everybody that needs a job oughta have one? An' anyway, right then he was listenin' to me, if ya can picture it. I'm makin' 'im feel better, I can tell. I'm sayin' how it's the same fer other men, an' he likes that, 'specially when I mention Harry Weinman, Sammy never liked him one bit. So I keep on talkin', an' for one minute, it's like we're kids again, feelin' close an' warm, him hangin' on to me, lettin' me rock 'im almost. An' listenin', listenin' to what I have to say. Like years ago when we lost little Bennie an' Sammy's ma an' Aunt Minnie, God rest 'em, one right after another....

I shoulda known, I shoulda seen it comin', but I kept on talkin'. Once ya get the chance, ya know, ya wanna git it all in. By this time he was blowin' his nose on that old rag of a hanky I got him, musta been four Chirstmases ago. An' silly me, I'm feelin' like a girl again, like I'm doin' somethin' big. Talkin' nice 'n easy, but strong, ya know, hearin' Ma and Bea in my ears. Givin' 'im somethin' he needs 'sides food an' a pair of mended socks. Never needed much from me 'cept what a man needs from a woman an' then to keep my mouth shut when his was open. Which was mosta the time.

An' ya know, holdin' him that way I started feelin' happy, not on accounta him cryin', just from bein' close like that again.

Sammy, I says, we're lucky, ya know. The kids're grown up an' on their own. They're doin' okay, as good as anybody. We're doin' okay, too, ya know. We ain't starvin' yet, an' we ain't goin' to.

Sammy, I says, lemme go back to washin'?

I say it real quiet. First he just looks at me, quiet too, like he's takin' it in, nice. And I'm thinkin', maybe this is it now, maybe he's come to his senses after all. So I go on.

Again I say, Sammy, I can take in some money washin'. Time hangs on me now, the kids been gone a long time, ya know.

Still he don't say a word, he's holdin' on to me, snifflin'. But somethin' changes in the air. I can feel it, but there's no turnin' back.

Sammy, things is hard all over, I says, but there's still some folks payin' for washin'. Why, Bea was tellin' me—

Well, that was it, couldn't say another word. There's Bea standin' in between us again wearin' horns an' a pitchfork. Always been that way. If I ain't to blame fer what's wrong, then Bea's to blame—just for bein'. There goes that snap in his eyes, like the gas when it comes up to flame. I was in for it now, fer sure.

That goddamned Bea, he says an' jerks in his tracks like somebody pulled the bit. She's fillin' yer head with bullshit again, ain't she?

An' then he was off. Rips away from me, an' starts

struttin' around the kitchen like that wind-up mouse we use to have for the kids, mockin' Bea, mockin' her deep voice from too much smokin', mockin' me how he heard me answer her. Makin' it all cheap an' small.

Pretty soon it was my fault we needed money, my fault he couldn't find no job, my fault for hangin' on 'im all these years, me an' the kids, my fault he could never get ahead. By the time he finished, it was my fault there was a Great Depression, an' if I'd just get the hell out of the country, FDR could see his way clear to endin' it, once an' fer all.

Well, now it's back to normal, him yellin' an' me listenin'. Then goes a snap again, but this time it's inside a me. Like a bolt a lightnin' it comes clear—I *ain't* the one that's crazy here. An' by God, a storm starts howlin' inside a me like I ain't never felt before. Good thing there was no knives lyin' around.

So I says to him, I'm no old rag, I says. I got wrinkles, my bones creak sometimes, an' I lost another tooth this year, I says, walking at 'im all the time til he's up against the wall with his eyes like baseballs. I ain't yer rag to wipe the floor with, I says. I worked hard an' I done a good job with my house an' kids an' I done a good job with you. Now you treat me like a person. Or you won't treat me at all.

Well, ya know he never said one single god-blessed word. Slid away from me like a snake along the wall. I was still yellin' when the door shut behind 'im. An' ya know what I done then? Just as if it was planned for a month a Sundays, I set about doin' what had to be done. By the time he come back that night, his clothes was all bundled up in the hall, the door hooked tight on the inside. I hear 'im coughin' out there, but he don't knock an' I don't open.

An' then he's gone, thirty-six years gone with 'im.

Now I know the man was crazy, throwin' over a good thing like that. Pushin' me to it all the time, beggin' me to ask 'im out the door. I figure it woulda gone this way no matter what I done. An' I ain't no rag doll to pull an' bend an' rip the stuffin' outta. Still I felt bad, like I done wrong not lettin' him stomp on me again. It's a damn shame, though. Coulda had some good years, thinkin' a just ourselves fer a change.

I dunno, maybe it was only me that seen his mean streak. He was a charmer too, that's fer sure. But since he lost his job, you could set a clock by his fits. I guess a man needs a steady job to feel good. Times like this, you take what ya can git. They ain't like us, ya know, able to git through a day just doin' what needs to be done. Sure, plenty a mornin's I wished I was goin' out the door with 'im, 'steada stayin' home wipin' floors an' noses. But what's yer lot in life, ya do, an' forget the fancy ideas.

I was just about crazy in the head at first, settin' up waitin' fer him to come home. Walkin' into the kitchen scared like his ghost was gonna pop out at me. Didn't know where he went, worried sick about 'im til Bea an' Tom seen 'im one day, all tight-lipped 'bout where he hangs his hat. Must be some young thing took him in, an' him gone nuts enough to do it. Fer awhile I wished he'd come back an' beg me to forgive 'im. But what the hell, he's too damn proud an' I'm too damn mad. After that I got kinda light-headed, like a kid, but that didn't last long neither. Now I just feel settled, done with it, like the way ya feel 'bout raisin' kids an' then they're gone.

By the way, I got work doin' washin' now. An' Mrs. Bennett's gonna recommend me to her ladyfriend next door. I leave the house early in the mornin'—just like he use to—an' I'm back fer coffee with Bea by the middle a the afternoon. If I don't feel like supper, I don't eat none. An' if I like to eat with friends, there's plenty a company around.

He might come back yet, Bea says, ya never know. But I seen the way she looks at me when I get my coat to go see Emily or Effie down the block, an' there she is cookin' at the stove.

Oh, I can't say there ain't no hard times. Thirty-six years ain't easy to put aside. Lookit yesterday. Went out marchin' with Emily an' Bill, come back feelin' like a spring chicken again. Then all of a sudden I'm cryin' like there ain't gonna be no time for it tomorrow.... Well. Cryin' fer dreams is somethin' I guess don't ever end.

Christmas Eve at Johnson's Drugs N Goods

Toni Cade Bambara

I was probably the first to spot them cause I'd been watching the entrance to the store on the lookout for my daddy, knowing that if he didn't show soon, he wouldn't be coming at all. His new family would be expecting him to spend the holidays with them. For the first half of my shift, I'd raced the cleaning cart down the aisles doing a slapdash job on the signs and glass cages, eager to stay in view of the doorway. And look like Johnson's kept getting bigger, swelling, sprawling itself all over the corner lot, just to keep me from the door, to wear me out in the marathon vigil.

In point of fact, Johnson's Drugs N Goods takes up less than one-third of the block. But it's laid out funny in crisscross aisles so you get to feeling like a rat in an endless maze. Plus the ceilings are high and the fluorescents a blazing white. And Mrs. Johnson's got these huge signs sectioning off the spaces—TOBACCO DRUGS HOUSEWARES, etc.—like it was some big-time department store. The thing is, till the two noisy women came in, it felt like a desert under a blazing sun. Piper in Tobacco even had on shades. The new dude in Drugs looked like he was at the end of a wrong-way telescope. I got to feeling like a nomad with the cleaning cart, trekking across the sands with no end in sight, wandering. The overhead lights creating mirages and racing up my heart till I'd realize that wasn't my daddy in the parking lot, just the poster-board Santa Claus. Or that wasn't my daddy in the entrance way, just the Burma Shave man in a frozen stance. Then I'd tried to make out pictures of Daddy getting off the bus at the terminal, or driving a rented car past the Chamber of Commerce building, or sitting jammed-leg in one of them DC point-o-nine brand X planes, coming to see me.

By the time the bus pulled into the lot and the two women in their big-city clothes hit the door, I'd decided Daddy was already at the house waiting for me, knowing that for a mirage too, since Johnson's is right across from the railroad and bus terminals and the house is a dollar-sixty cab away. And I know he wouldn't feature going to the house on the off chance of running into Mama. Or even if he escaped that fate, having to sit in the parlor with his hat in his lap while Aunt Harriet looks him up and down grunting, too busy with the latest crossword puzzle contest to offer the man some supper. And Uncle Henry talking a blue streak bout how he outfoxed the city council or somethin and nary a cold beer in sight for my daddy.

But then the two women came banging into the store and I felt better. Right away the store stopped sprawling, got fixed. And we all got pulled together from our various zones to one focal point—them. Changing up the whole atmosphere of the place fore they even got into the store proper. Before we knew it, we were all smiling, looking halfway like you supposed to on Christmas Eve, even if you do got to work for ole lady Johnson, who don't give you no slack whatever the holiday.

"What the hell does this mean, Ethel?" the one in the fur coat say, talking loud and fast, yanking on the rails that lead the way into the store. "What are we, cattle? Being herded into the blankety-blank store and in my fur coat," she grumbles, boosting herself up between the rails, swinging her body along like the kids do in the park.

Me and Piper look at each other and smile. Then Piper moves down to the edge of the counter right under the Tobacco sign so as not to miss nothing. Madeen over in Housewares waved to me to ask what's up and I just shrug. I'm fascinated by the women.

"Look here," the one called Ethel say, drawing the words out lazy slow. "Do you got a token for this sucker?" She's shoving hard against the turnstile folks supposed to exit through. Pushing past and grunting, the turnstile crank cranking like it gonna bust, her Christmas corsage of holly and bells just ajingling and hanging by a thread. Then she gets through and stumbles toward the cigar counter and leans back against it, studying the turnstile hard. It whips back around in place, making scrunching noises like it's been abused.

"You know one thing," she say, dropping her face onto her coat collar so Piper'd know he's being addressed.

"Ma'am?"

"That is one belligerent bad boy, that thing right there."

Piper laughs his prizewinning laugh and starts touching the stacks of gift-wrapped stuff, case the ladies in the market for pipe tobacco or something. Two or three of the customers who'd been falling asleep in the magazines coming to life now, inching forward. Phototropism, I'd call it, if somebody asked me for a word.

The one in the fur coat's coming around now the right way—if you don't count the stiff-elbow rail-walking she was doing—talking about "Oh, my God, I can walk, I can walk, Ethel, praise de lawd."

The two women watching Piper touch the cigars, the humidors, the gift-wrapped boxes. Mostly he's touching himself, cause George Lee Piper love him some George Lee Piper. Can't blame him. Piper be fine.

"You work on commissions, young man?" Fur Coat asking.

"No, ma'am."

The two women look at each other. They look over toward the folks inching forward. They look at me gliding by with the cleaning cart. They look back at each other and shrug.

"So what's his problem?" Ethel says in a stage whisper. "Why he so hot to sell us something?"

"Search me." Fur Coat starts flapping her coat and frisking herself. "You know?" she asking me.

"It's a mystery to me," I say, doing my best to run ole man Samson over. He sneaking around trying to jump Madeen in Housewares. And it is a mystery to me how come Piper always so eager to make a sale. You'd think he had half interest in the place. He says it's because it's his job, and after all, the Johnsons are Black folks. I guess so, I guess so. Me, I just clean the place and stay busy in case Mrs. J is in the prescription booth, peeking out over the top of the glass.

When I look around again, I see that the readers are suddenly very interested in cigars. They crowding around Ethel and Fur Coat. Piper kinda embarrassed by all the attention, though fine as he is, he oughta be used to it. His expression's cool but his hands give him away, sliding around the counter like he shuffling a deck of slippery cards. Fur Coat nudges Ethel and they bend over to watch the hands, doing these chicken-head jerkings. The readers take up positions just like a director was hollering "Places" at em. Piper, never one to disappoint an audience, starts zipping around these invisible walnut shells. Right away Fur Coat whips out a little red change purse and slaps a dollar bill on the counter. Ethel dips deep into her coat pocket, bending her knees and being real comic, then plunks down some change. Ole man Sampson tries to boost up on my cleaning cart to see the shells that ain't there.

"Scuse me, Mr. Sampson," I say, speeding the cart up sudden so that quite naturally he falls off, the dirty dog.

Piper is snapping them imaginary shells around like nobody's business, one of the readers leaning over another's shoulder, staring pop-eyed.

"All right now, everybody step back," Ethel announces. She waves the crowd back and pushes up one coat sleeve, lifts her fist into the air and jerks out one stiff finger from the bunch, and damn if the readers don't lift their heads to behold in amazement this wondrous finger.

"That, folks," Fur Coat explains, "is what is known as the indicator finger. The indicator is about to indicate the indicatee."

"Say wha?" Dirty ole man Sampson decides he'd rather sneak up on Madeen than watch the show.

"What's going on over there?" Miz Della asks me. I spray the watch case and make a big thing of wiping it and ignoring her. But then the new dude in Drugs hollers over the same thing.

"Christmas cheer gone to the head. A coupla vaudevillians," I say. He smiles, and Miz Della says "Ohhh" like I was talking to her.

"This one," Ethel says, planting a finger exactly one-quarter of an inch from the countertop.

Piper dumb-shows a lift of the shell, turning his face away as though he can't bear to look and find the elusive pea ain't there and he's gonna have to take the ladies' money. Then his eyes swivel around and sneak a peek and widen, lighting up his whole face in a prizewinning grin.

"You got it," he shouts.

The women grab each other by the coat shoulders and jump each other up and down. And I look toward the back cause I know Mrs. J got to be hearing all this carrying-on, and on payday if Mr. J ain't handing out the checks, she's going to give us some long lecture about decorum and what it means to be on board at Johnson's Drugs N Goods. I wheel over to the glass jars and punch bowls, wanting alibi distance just in case. And also to warn Madeen about Sampson gaining on her. He's ducking down behind the coffeepots, walking squat and shameless.

"Pay us our money, young man," Fur Coat is demanding, rapping her knuckles on the counter.

"Yeah, what kind of crooked shell game is you running here in this joint?" say Ethel, finding a good foil character to play.

"We should hate to have to turn the place out, young man."

"It out," echoes Ethel.

The women nod to the crowd and a coupla folks giggle. And Piper tap-taps on the cash register like he shonuff gonna give em they money. I'd rather they turned the place out myself. I want to call my daddy. Only way any of us are going to get home in time to dress for the Christmas dance at the center is for the women to turn it out. Like I say, Piper ain't too clear about the worker's interest versus management's, as the dude in Drugs would say it. So he's light-tapping and quite naturally the cash drawer does not come out. He's yanking some unseen dollar from the not-there drawer and handing it over. Damn if Fur Coat don't snatch it, deal out the bills to herself and her friend and then make a big production out of folding the money flat and jamming it in that little red change purse.

"I wanna thank you," Ethel says, strolling off, swinging her pocketbook so that the crowd got to back up and disperse. Fur Coat spreads her coat and curtsies.

"A pleasure to do business with you ladies," Piper says, tipping his hat, looking kinda disappointed that he didn't sell em something. Tipping his hat the way he tipped the shells, cause you know Mrs. J don't allow no hats indoors. I came to work in slacks one time and she sent me home to change and docked me too. I wear a gele some times just to mess her around, and you can tell she trying to figure out if she'll go for it or not. The woman is crazy. Not Uncle Henry type crazy, but Black property owner type crazy. She thinks this is a museum, which is why folks don't hardly come in here to shop. That's okay cause we all get to know each other well. It's not okay cause it's a drag to look busy. If you look like you ain't buckling under a weight of work, Mrs. J will have you count the Band-Aids in the boxes to make sure the company ain't pulling a fast one. The woman crazy.

Now Uncle Henry type crazy is my kind of crazy. The type crazy to get you a job. He march into the "saloon" as he calls it and tells Leon D that he is not an equal opportunity employer and that he, Alderman Henry Peoples, is going to put some fire to his ass. So soon's summer comes, me and Madeen got us a job at Leon D. Salon. One of them hushed, funeral type shops with skinny models parading around for customers corseted and strangling in their seats, huffin and puffin.

Madeen got fired right off on account of the pound of mascara she wears on each lash and them weird dresses she designs for herself (with less than a yard of cloth each if you ask me). I did my best to hang in there so's me and Madeen'd have hang-around money till Johnson started hiring again. But it was hard getting back and forth from the stockroom to this little kitchen to fix the espresso to the showroom. One minute up to your ass in carpet, the next skidding across white linoleum, the next making all this noise on ceramic tile and people looking around at you and all. Was there for two weeks and just about had it licked by stationing different kind of shoes at each place that I could slip into, but then Leon D stumbled over my bedroom slippers one afternoon.

But to hear Uncle Henry tell it, writing about it all to Daddy, I was working at a promising place making a name for myself. And Aunt Harriet listening to Uncle Henry read the letter, looking me up and down and grunting. She know what kind of name it must be, cause my name in the family is Miss Clumsy. Like if you got a glass-top coffee table with doodads on em, or a hurricane lamp sitting on a mantel anywhere near a door I got to come through, or an antique jar you brought all the way from Venice the time you won the crossword puzzle contest—you can rest assure I'll demolish them by and by. I ain't vicious, I'm just clumsy. It's my gawky stage, Mama says. Aunt Harriet cuts her eye at Mama and grunts.

My daddy advised me on the phone not to mention anything to the Johnsons about this gift of mine for disaster or the fact that I worked at Leon D. Salon. No sense the Johnson's calling up there to check on me and come to find I knocked over a perfume display two times in the same day. Like I say—it's a gift. So when I got to clean the glass jars and punch bowls at Johnson's, I take it slow and pay attention. Then I take up my station relaxed in Fabrics, where the worst that can happen is I upset a box of pins.

Mrs. J is in the prescription booth, and she clears her throat real loud. We all look to the back to read the smoke signals. She ain't paying Fur Coat and Ethel no attention. They over in Cosmetics messing with Miz Della's mind and her customers. Mrs. J got her eye on some young teenagers browsing around Jewelry. The other eye on Piper. But this does not mean Piper is supposed to check the kids out. It means Madeen is. You got to know how to read Mrs. J to get along.

She always got one eye on Piper. Tries to make it seem like she don't trust him at the cash register. That may be part of the reason now, now that she's worked up this cover story so in her mind. But we all know why she watches Piper, same reason we all do. Cause Piper is so fine you just can't help yourself. Tall and built up, blue-black and smooth, got the nerve to have dimples, and wears this splayed-out push-broom mustache he's always raking in with three fingers. Got a big butt too that makes you wanna hug the customer that asks for the cartoons Piper keeps behind him, two shelfs down. Mercy. And when it's slow, or when Mrs. J comes bustling over for the count, Piper steps from behind the counter and shows his self. You get to see the whole Piper from the shiny boots to the glistening fro and every inch of him fine. Enough to make you holler.

Miz Della in Cosmetics, a sister who's been passing for years but fooling nobody but herself, she always lolligagging over to Tobacco talking bout are there any new samples of those silver-tipped cigars for women. Piper don't even squander energy to bump her off any more. She mostly just ain't even there. At first he would get mad when she used to act hinkty and had these white men picking her up at the store. Then he got sorrowful about it all, saying she was a pitiful person. Now that she's going out with the blond chemist back there, he just wiped her off the map. She tries to mess with him, but Piper ain't heard the news she's been born. Sometimes his act slips, though, cause he does take a lot of unnecessary energy to play up to Madeen whenever Miz Della's hanging around. He's not consistent in his attentions, and that spurs Madeen the dress designer to madness. And Piper really oughta put brakes on that, cause Madeen subject to walk in one day in a fishnet dress and no underwear and then what he goin do about that?

Last year on my birthday my daddy got on us about dressing like hussies to attract the boys. Madeen shrugged it off and went about her business. It hurt my feelings. The onliest reason I was wearing that tight sweater and that skimpy skirt was cause I'd been to the roller rink and that's how we dress. But my daddy didn't even listen and I was really hurt. But then later that night, I come through the living room to make some cocoa and he apologized. He lift up from the couch where he always sleeps when he comes to visit, lifted up and whispered it—"Sorry." I could just make him out by the light from the refrigerator.

"Candy," he calls to make sure I heard him. And I don't want to close the frig door cause I know I'll want to remember this scene, figuring it's going to be the last birthday visit cause he fixin to get married and move outta state.

"Sir?"

He pat the couch and I come on over and just leave the frig door open so we can see each other. I forgot to put the milk down, so I got this cold milk bottle in my lap, feeling stupid.

"I was a little rough on you earlier," he say, picking something I can't see from my bathrobe. "But you're getting to be a woman now and certain things have to be said. Certain things have to be understood so you can decide what kind of woman you're going to be, ya know?"

"Sir," I nod. I'm thinking Aunt Harriet ought to tell me, but then Aunt Harriet prefers to grunt at folks, reserving words for the damn crossword puzzles. And my mama stay on the road so much with the band, when she do come home for a hot minute all she has to tell me is "My slippers're in the back closet" or "Your poor tired Ma'd like some coffee."

He takes my hand and don't even kid me about the milk bottle, just holds my hand for a long time saying nothing, just squeezes it. And I know he feeling bad about moving away and all, but what can he do, he got a life to lead. Just like Mama got her life to lead. Just like I got my life to lead and'll probably leave here myself one day and become an actress or a director. And I know I should tell him it's all right. Sitting there with that milk bottle chilling me through my bathrobe, the light from the refrigerator throwing funny shadows on the wall, I know that years later when I'm in trouble or something, or hear that my daddy died or something like that, I'm going feel real bad that I didn't tell him—it's all right, Daddy, I understand. It ain't like he'd made any promises about making a home for me with him. So it ain't like he's gone back on his word. And if the new wife can't see taking in no half-grown new daughter, hell, I understand that. I can't get the words together, neither can he. So we just squeeze each other's hands. And that'll have to do.

"When I was a young man," he says after while, "there were girls who ran around all made up in sassy clothes. And they were okay to party with, but not the kind you cared for, ya know?" I nod and he pats my hand. But I'm thinking that ain't right, to party with a person you don't care for. How come you can't? I want to ask, but he's talking. And I was raised not to interrupt folk when they talking, especially my daddy. "You and Madeen cause quite a stir down at the barbershop." He tries to laugh it, but it comes out scary. "Got to make up your mind now what kind of woman you're going to be. You know what I'm saying?" I nod and he loosens his grip so I can go make my cocoa.

I'm messing around in the kitchenette feeling dishonest. Things I want to say, I haven't said. I look back over toward the couch and know this picture is going to haunt me later. Going to regret the things left unsaid. Like a coward, like a child maybe. I fix my cocoa and keep my silence, but I do remember to put the milk back and close the refrigerator door.

"Candy?"

"Sir?" I'm standing there in the dark, the frig door

closed now and we can't even see each other.

"It's not about looks anyway," he says, and I hear him settling deep into the couch and pulling up the bedclothes. "And it ain't always about attracting some man either ... not necessarily.

I'm waiting to hear what it is about, the cup shaking in the saucer and me wanting to ask him all over again how it was when he and Mama first met in Central Park, and how it used to be when they lived in Philly and had me and how it was when the two of them were no longer making any sense together but moved down here anyway and then split up. But I could hear that breathing he does just before the snoring starts. So I hustle on down the hall so I won't be listening for it and can't get to sleep.

All night I'm thinking about this woman I'm going to be. I'll look like Mama but don't wanna be no singer. Was named after Grandma Candestine but don't wanna be no fussy old woman with a bunch of kids. Can't see myself turning into Aunt Harriet either, doing crossword puzzles all day long. I look over at Madeen, all sprawled out in her bed, tangled up in the sheets looking like the alcoholic she trying to be these days, sneaking liquor from Uncle Henry's closet. And I know I don't wanna be stumbling down the street with my boobs out and my dress up and my heels cracking off and all. I write for a whole hour in my diary trying to connect with the future me and trying not to hear my daddy snoring.

Fur Coat and Ethel in Housewares talking with Madeen. I know they must be cracking on Miz Della, cause I hear Madeen saying something about equal opportunity. We used to say that Mrs. J was an equal opportunity employer for hiring Miz Della. But then she went and hired real white folks—a blond, crew-cut chemist and a pimply-face kid for the stockroom. If you ask me, that's running equal opportunity in the ground. And running the business underground cause don't nobody round here deal with no white chemist. They used to wrinkly old folks grinding up the herbs and bark and telling them very particular things to do and not to do working the roots. So they keep on going to Mama Drear down past the pond or Doc Jessup in back of the barbershop. Don't do a doctor one bit of good to write out a prescription talking about fill it at Johnson's, cause unless it's an emergency folk stay strictly away from a white root worker, especially if he don't tell you what he doing.

Aunt Harriet in here one day when Mama Drear was too sick to counsel and quite naturally she asks the chemist to explain what all he doing back there with the mortar and pestle and the scooper and the scales. And he say something about rules and regulations, the gist of which was mind your business, lady. Aunt Harriet dug down deep into her crossword-puzzle words and pitched a natural bitch. Called that man a bunch of choicest names. But the line that got me was—"Medication without explanation is obscene." And what she say that for, we ran that in the ground for days. Infatuation without fraternization is obscene. Insemination without obligation is tyranny. Fornication without contraception is obtuse, and so forth and so on. Madeen's best line came out the night we were watching a TV special about welfare. Sterilization without strangulation and hell's damnation is I-owe-you-one-crackers. Look like every situation called for a line like that, and even if it didn't, we made it fit.

Then one Saturday morning we were locked out and we standing around shivering in our sweaters and this old white dude jumps out a pickup truck hysterical, his truck still in gear and backing out the lot. His wife had given their child an overdose of medicine and the kid was out cold. Look like everything he said was grist for the mill.

"She just administered the medicine without even reading the label," he told the chemist, yanking on his jacket so the man couldn't even get out his keys. "She never even considered the fact it might be dangerous, the medicine so old and all." We follow the two down the aisle to the prescription booth, the old white dude talking a mile a minute, saying they tried to keep the kid awake, tried to walk him, but he wouldn't walk. Tried to give him an enema, but he wouldn't stay propped up. Could the chemist suggest something to empty his stomach out and sooth his inflamed ass and what all? And besides he was breathing funny and should he administer mouth-to-mouth resuscitation? The minute he tore out of there and ran down the street to catch up with his truck, we started in.

Administration without consideration is illiterate. Irrigation without resuscitation is evacuation without ambulation is inflammation without information is execution without restitution is. We got downright silly about the whole thing till Mrs. J threatened to fire us all. But we kept it up for a week.

Then the new dude in Drugs who don't never say much stopped the show one afternoon when we were trying to figure out what to call the street riots in the sixties and so forth. He say Revolution without Transformation is Half-assed. Took me a while to ponder that one, a whole day in fact just to work up to it. After while I would listen real hard whenever he opened his mouth, which wasn't often. And I jotted down the titles of the books I'd see him with. And soon's I finish up the stack that's by my bed, I'm hitting the library. He started giving me some of the newspapers he keeps stashed in that blue bag of his we all at first thought was full of funky jockstraps and sneakers. Come to find it's full of carrots and oranges and books and stuff. Madeen say he got a gun in there too. But then Madeen all the time saying something. Like she saying here lately that the chemist's jerking off there behind the poisons and the goopher dust.

The chemist's name is Hubert Tarrly. Madeen tagged him Herbert Tareyton. But the name that stuck was Nazi Youth. Every time I look at him I hear Hitler barking out over the loudspeaker urging the youth to measure up and take over the world. And I can see these stark-eyed gray kids in short pants and suspenders doing jump-ups and scissor kicks and turning they mamas in to the Gestapo for listening to the radio. Chemist looks like he grew up like that, eating knockwurst and beating on Jews, rounding up gypsies, saying *Sieg heil* and shit. Mrs. J said something to him one morning and damn if he didn't click his heels. I like to die. She blushing all over her simple self talking bout that's Southern cavalier style. I could smell the gas. I could see the flaming cross too. Nazi Youth and then some. The dude in Drugs started calling him that too, the dude whose name I can never remember. I always wanna say Ali Baba when I talk about him with my girl friends down at the skating rink or with the older sisters at the arts center. But that ain't right. Either you call a person a name that says what they about or you call em what they call themselves, one or the other.

Now take Fur Coat, for instance. She is clearly about the fur coat. She moving up and down the aisles talking while Ethel in the cloth coat is doing all the work, picking up teapots, checking the price on the dust mops, clicking a bracelet against the punch bowl to see if it ring crystal, hollering to somebody about whether the floor wax need buffing or not. And it's all on account of the fur coat. Her work is something other than that. Like when they were in Cosmetics messing with Miz Della, some white ladies come up talking about what's the latest in face masks. And every time Miz Della pull something out the box, Ethel shake her head and say that brand is crap. Then Fur Coat trots out the sure-fire recipe for the face mask. What she tells the old white ladies is to whip up some egg white to peaks, pour in some honey, some oil of wintergreen, some oil of eucalyptus, the juice of a lemon and a half a teaspoon of arsenic. Now any fool can figure out what lemon juice do to arsenic, or how honey going make the concoction stick, and what all else the oil of this and that'll do to your face. But Fur Coat in her fur coat make you stand still and listen to this madness. Fur Coat an authority in her fur coat. The fur coat is an act of alchemy in itself, as Aunt Harriet would put it.

Just like my mama in her fur coat, same kind too—Persian lamb, bought hot in some riot or other. Mama's coat was part of the Turn the School Out Outfit. Hardly ever came out of the quilted bag cept for that. Wasn't for window-shopping, wasn't for going to rehearsal, wasn't for church teas, was for working her show. She'd flip a flap of that coat back over her hip when she strolled into the classroom to get on the teacher's case bout saying something out of the way about Black folks. Then she'd pick out the exact plank, exact spot she'd take her stand on, then plant one of them black suede pumps from the I. Miller outlet she used to work at. Then she'd lift her chin arrogant proud to start the rap, and all us kids would lean forward and stare at the cameo brooch visible now on the wide-wale wine plush corduroy dress. Then she'd work her show in her outfit. Bam-bam that black suede pocketbook punctuating the points as Mama ticked off the teacher's offenses. And when she got to the good part, and all us kids would strain up off the benches to hear every word so we could play it out in the schoolyard, she'd take both fists and brush that fur coat way back past her hips and she'd challenge the teacher to either change up and apologize or meet her for a showdown at a school-board hearing. And of course ole teacher'd apologize to all us Black kids. Then Mama'd let the coat fall back into place and she'd whip around, the coat draping like queen robes, and march herself out. Mama was baad in her fur coat.

I don't know what-all Fur Coat do in her fur coat but I can tell it's hellafying whatever it all is. They came into Fabrics and stood around a while trying to see what shit they could get into. All they had in their baskets was a teapot and some light bulbs and some doodads from the special gift department, perfume and whatnot. I waited on a few customers wanting braid and balls of macramé twine, nothing where I could show my stuff. Now if somebody wanted some of the silky, juicy cotton stuff I could get into something fancy, yanking off the yards, measuring it doing a shuffle-stick number, nicking it just so, then ripping the hell out the shit. But didn't nobody ask for that. Fur Coat and Ethel kinda finger some bolts and trade private jokes, then they moved onto Drugs.

"We'd like to see the latest in rubberized fashions for men, young man." Fur Coat is doing a super Lady Granville Whitmore the Third number. "If you would." She bows her head, fluttering her lashes.

Me and Madeen start messing around in the shoe-polish section so's not to miss nothing. I kind of favor Fur Coat, on account of she got my mama's coat on, I guess. On the other hand, I like the way Ethel drawl talk like she too tired and bored to go on. I guess I like em both cause they shopping the right way, having fun and all. And they got plenty of style. I wouldn't mind being like that when I am full-grown.

The dude in Drugs thinks on the request a while, sucking in his lips like he wanna talk to himself on the inside. He's looking up and down the counter, pauses at the plastic rain hats, rejects them, then squints hard at Ethel and Fur Coat. Fur Coat plants a well-helled foot on the shelf with the tampons and pads and sighs. Something about that sigh I don't like. It's real rather than play snooty. The dude in Drugs always looks a little crumbled, a little rough dry, like he jumped straight out the hamper but not quite straight. But he got stuff to him if you listen rather than look. Seems to me ole Fur Coat is looking. She keeps looking while the dude moves down the aisle behind the counter, ducks down out of sight, reappears and comes back, dumping an armful of boxes on the counter.

"One box of Trojans and one box of Ramses," Ethel announces. "We want to do the comparison test."

"On the premises?" Lady G Fur says, planting a dignified hand on her collarbone.

"Egg-zack-lee."

"In your opinion, young man," Lady G Fur says, staying the arm of the brand tester, "which of the two is the best? Uhmm—the better of the two, that is. In your vast experience as lady-killer and cock hound, which passes the X test?" It's said kinda snotty. Me and Madeen exchange a look and dust around the cans of shoe polish.

"Well," the dude says, picking up a box in each hand,

"in my opinion, Trojans have a snappier ring to em." He rattles the box against his ear, then lets Ethel listen. She nods approval. Fur Coat will not be swayed. "On the other hand, Ramses is a smoother smoke. Cooler on the throat. What do you say in your vast experience as—er—"

Ethel is banging down boxes of Kotex cracking up, screaming, "He gotcha. He gotcha that time. Old laundry bag got over on you, Helen."

Mrs. J comes out of the prescription booth and hustles her bulk to the counter. Me and Madeen clamp down hard on giggles and I damn near got to climb in with the neutral shoe polish to escape attention. Ethel and Fur Coat don't give a shit, they paying customers, so they just roar. Cept Fur Coat's roar is phony, like she really mad and gonna get even with the dude for not turning out to be a chump. Meanwhile, the dude is standing like a robot, arms out at exactly the same height, elbows crooked just so, boxes displayed between thumb and next finger, the gears in the wrist click, clicking, turning. And not even cracking a smile.

"What's the problem here?" Mrs. J trying not to sound breathless or angry and ain't doing too good a job. She got to say it twice to be heard.

"No problem, Mrs. Johnson," the dude says straight-face. "The customers are buying condoms, I am selling condoms. A sale is being conducted, as is customary in a store."

Mrs. J looks down at the jumble of boxes and covers her mouth. She don't know what to do. I duck down, cause when folks in authority caught in a trick, the first they look for is a scapegoat.

"Well, honey," Ethel says, giving a chummy shove to Mrs. J's shoulder, "what do you think? I've heard that Trojans are ultrasensitive. They use a baby lamb brain, I understand."

"Membrane, dear, membrane," Fur Coat says down her nose. "They remove the intestines of a four-week-old lamb and use the membrane. Tough, resilient, sheer."

"Gotcha," says Ethel. "On the other hand, it is said by folks who should know that Ramses has a better box score."

"Box score," echoes Mrs. J in a daze.

"Box score. You know, honey—no splits, breaks, leaks, seeps."

"Seepage, dear, seepage," says Fur Coat, all nasal.

"Gotcha."

"The solution," says the dude in an almost robot voice, "is to take one small box of each and do the comparison test as you say. A survey. A random sampling of your friends." He says this to Fur Coat, who is not enjoying it all nearly so much as Ethel, who is whooping and hollering.

Mrs. J backs off and trots to the prescription booth. Nazi Youth peeks over the glass and mumbles something soothing to Mrs. J. He waves me and Madeen away like he somebody we got to pay some mind.

"We will take one super-duper, jumbo family size of each."

"Family size?" Fur Coat is appalled. "And one more thing, young man," she orders. "Wrap up a petite size for a small-size smart-ass acquaintance of mine. Gift-wrapped, ribbons and all."

It occurs to me that Fur Coat's going to present this to the dude. Right then and there I decide I don't like her. She's not discriminating with her stuff. Up till then I was thinking how much I'd like to trade Aunt Harriet in for either of these two, hang out with them, sit up all night while they drink highballs and talk about men they've known and towns they've been in. I always did want to hang out with women like this and listen to their stories. But they beginning to reveal themselves as not nice people, just cause the dude is rough dry on Christmas Eve. My Uncle Henry all the time telling me they different kinds of folks in the community, but when you boil it right down there's just nice and not nice. Uncle Henry say they folks who'll throw they mamas to the wolves if the fish sandwich big enough. They folks who won't whatever the hot sauce. They folks that're scared folks that are dumb; folks that have heart and some with heart to spare. That all boils down to nice and not nice if you ask me. It occurs to me that Fur Coat is not nice. Fun, dazzling, witty, but not nice.

"Do you accept Christmas gifts, young man?" Fur Coat asking in icy tones she ain't masking too well.

"No. But I do accept Kwanza presents at the feast."

"Quan ... hmm..."

Fur Coat and Ethel go into a huddle with the stage whispers. "I bet he thinks we don't know beans about Quantas ... Don't he know we are The Ebony Jet Set ... We never travel to kangaroo land except by..."

Fur Coat straightens up and stares at the dude. "Will you accept a whatchamacallit gift from me even though we are not feasting, as it were?"

"If it is given with love and respect, my sister, of course." He was sounding so sincere, it kinda got to Fur Coat.

"In that case..." She scoops up her bundle and sweeps out the place. Ethel trotting behind hollering, "He gotcha, Helen. Give the boy credit. Maybe we should hire him and do a threesome act." She spun the turnstile round three times for she got into the spin and spun out the store.

"Characters," says Piper on tiptoe, so we all can hear him. He laughs and checks his watch. Madeen slinks over to Tobacco to be in asking distance in case he don't already have a date to the dance. Miz Della's patting some powder on. I'm staring at the door after Fur Coat and Ethel, coming to terms with the fact that my daddy ain't coming. It's gonna be just Uncle Henry and Aunt Harriet this year, with maybe Mama calling on the phone between sets to holler in my ear, asking have I been a good girl, it's been that long since she's taken a good look at me.

"You wanna go to the Kwanza celebrations with me sometime this week or next week, Candy?"

I turn and look at the dude. I can tell my face is falling and right now I don't feel up to doing anything about it. Holidays are depressing. Maybe there's something joyous about this celebration he's talking about. Cause Lord knows Christmas is a drag. The sister who taught me how to wrap a gele asked me was I coming to the celebration down at the Black Arts Center, but I didn't know nothing bout it.

"Look here," I finally say, "would you please get a pencil and paper and write your name down for me. And write that other word down too so I can look it up."

He writes his name down and spins the paper around for me to read.

"Obatale."

"Right," he says, spinning it back. "But you can call me Ali Baba if you want to." He was leaning over too far writing out Kwanza for me to see if that was a smile on his face or a smirk. I figure a smile, cause Obatale nice people.

One Summer

Yvonne Pepin

June 16

One orange ember peeks out at me from underneath a gray blanket of ash. I move back and forth in the old maple rocker in front of the fire and fish drowned gnats from my wine cup. The insects were enticed, dazed, then scorched by the kerosene lamp. Firelight flashes out from behind the stove grate onto the log walls and makes the cabin glow for my first night home in six months.

My first day back and already I've set up my easel on the porch so I can paint and look down on the clear sheets of creek waters. My studio lighting is controlled by the sun's arch across the sky. The porch roof covers me. The

---

Excerpted from *Three Summers: A Journal* (Shameless Hussy Press)

floor boards that support me remain as solid as the Oregon mountains surrounding me.

I've made a list of all the things I want to accomplish this summer. When I reread it, I had to cross out some things and hone it to this:

1. commune with nature
2. relearn about the wilds and myself
3. study the moon
4. raise the studio walls
5. drawknife wall logs
6. paint
7. do illustrations and articles
8. write up my color studies
9. read
10. build book shelves
11. clear the woods
12. cut firewood
13. re-lay the sink drain
14. build a wood shed
15. paint the moon

June 18

I celebrate my homecoming with the beginning of my menstrual cycle and the full moon. I am reclaiming, re-identifying with strengths, insights and portions of myself that have remained dormant for so many months. Silence and space open me to the silent space inside of me.

This morning I finished unpacking and storing food. The afternoon found me running the mountainsides, singing, dancing. When the afternoon shadows began to lengthen on the mountainsides, I returned to the cabin.

I dug up the sink drain pipe and laid it deeper in the ground, covering it with grass, hoping it wouldn't freeze.

Pick and dig. My muscles began to speak. I felt a sense of totality, knowing I can provide for myself on many levels.

At sunset I ran up the mountain and traversed it westwardly until I came to the ancient ponderosa pine snag. I squatted beneath it and sang my made-up mountain chant. A goshawk perched on the snag's top limb. In my mind I painted the scene, the goshawk in the snag, because after a full day I lacked the energy to record it in paint.

June 25

Today the only thoughts I want to know are my own. The only sounds I want to hear, from the elemental movements, my occasional song, Inipi's meow. Knowing is the silence I know. But the voices of others, friends and lovers, infiltrate my thoughts, take me from my single-mindedness. Perhaps this is the reason for community; so that we may all think together, listen together. In this way, our individualness cannot be cultivated or felt fully.

Last night, before sunset, I walked up the mountain to pick kinickinic. I took a bearing of southeast 30 degrees and blazed a steep line up the mountainside. I stopped to sketch the huge yellow-belly snag, the one I'd watched the goshawk in. Later, up the mountain a ways, I stopped to rest on a fallen pine. A goshawk swooped down at me, back and forth. I was afraid she was going to pick my eyes out, defending her territory I had unknowingly strayed into. She settled in a tree near me. I sang her a song about my reverence and appreciation for the beauty of this bird. I sketched as I watched her watch me. When she flew away, I continued my kinickinic quest.

She flew back, traversing the airway above my path. She cried out. I sang. Maybe she sang and I cried. Whatever, we established a communication; an earth-bound mortal, a lofty hunting bird, dialog.

June 26

The evening woods speak of a quality different than day. Light is less diffused, speckled instead against the trees, and lies in disassociated patches on the pine-needle- and branch-strewn floor. It is in the quiet of the evening that my eyes draw in what day's intensity washes out and the dark night obscures.

I read the trees. The leaners, snags, cull to loggers. I scan headlines of fir tips, tamarack, knobs, and pine cones. A goshawk twice as large as Inipi descends through a maze of trees onto the dead lower limbs of fir. I watch in silence, aware of her presence, she unaware of mine, until I begin to chant, softly at first, then with more voice until I gain all the attention of her jerky-necked hawk movements bobbing from the branch. She continues to stare, retracting and extending her head, a shrug of wing.

I don't think it is my place to find a place in a system; rather to exist and evolve from a situation that is spontaneous. I think it has to do with the spirit of matter, and that's why my place is not in a system, but alone, here in the mountains. A system is defined and planned according to matter which does not leave room for the spirit to breathe.

There is a lot to be said, though, for systems. They represent structure, the architectural underpinnings upon which technology has developed. Technology, when used to aid health and welfare, is technology used purposefully, to its fullest. But when the technological mind uses its power to create elements of warfare and planetary rape, then the system in which the mind has developed is detrimental toward natural systems.

The natural system, by my observations, moves by an ungraphable, invisible essence. The essence, or spirit, moves like wind, like wave, always in constant, expanding and retractable motion, sometimes at a lull, other times with great tidal impact.

My system cannot be defined. The beginning was my birth through which my body channels time until my death. My goal is not to know, or systematize or structure time to achieve, but to flow with the spirit of the earth.

I had really forgotten the frustration of having to cope entirely alone with every dilemma, until this afternoon when the hose to the bath house kept continually getting clogged. The high creek waters impaled clumps of sediment in the tubes, damming the gravity flow. No amount of blowing and sucking the disjoined hoses proved much help for long. No sooner would I siphon out the impediment than the hose would become clogged again.

On the last trip up the creek to disjoin the hoses and reposition them, I fell in the icy water and the section of hose I held floated like a snake downstream. Luckily, it got caught in a log jam and I retrieved it before it floated to the Pine Valley River.

After all this, my patience was as thin as a cirrus cloud, and I almost hyperventilated twice, blowing and sucking on the hose; so I did a rare thing: I quit pushing myself, went up to the cabin and ate lunch and continued to read May Sartons's *A Reckoning.*

In the novel, the main character, Laura, is dying of lung cancer. She says, "I have to do what I can and not count the cost. It's the last chance."

I feel, too, I must abide by this "last chance" philosophy and only put my soul through places that make me light.

June 28

The loneliest experience for me in living alone, the kind that hollows the marrow from my bone, leaving me empty, does not occur from the days spent without humans, but the opposite—going to town.

All around me in the market, laundromat, hardware store, are couples and families, pairs and circles. Then there is me. I feel an identification with the stray dog that wanders through the laundromat. It is mostly when I am around people that I feel their absence in my life, the need for intimacy and communication. Luckily the phone in town often connects me with familiarity. So it was like food that nourished my emptiness when I talked to R. long distance this afternoon. But I did not want to hang up, let go of this sustaining connection. Though 800 miles away now, R. fills some crucial need in my heart that is not favored in my solitary living. Perhaps this is why I painted the holes in the forest foliage this morning at dawn. All of nature gives me metaphors in which to understand my own life. The spaces between branch and bark beckoned me to explore the rich darkness of their emptiness.

Food is a problem for me; how to feed myself nutritious meals. Every time I push my silver cart through the grocery store, I become choked and confused. What to buy to eat? I ricochet, dumbfounded, between aisles of prepackaged, canned, wrapped, dried and fresh foods. By the time I reach the cashier I am sick to my stomach and on the verge of tears. This is what happened to me again in town this afternoon. And yet I always purchase the same things: cheese, crackers, cat food, lettuce and wine.

Driving out of town today, my spirit began to reclaim

familiar ground when gargantuan thunderheads in the sky drew me out of my depression. It was 95 degrees in the valley and sunny, but black in the northeast, the direction of the storm.

I pulled my truck into a small dirt turn-around and set up my French easel to paint these ethereal thunderheads, clouds like I've only seen in biblical paintings. It was essential to paint them from the east because the sun highlighted the clouds from this side to produce a heavenly radiance. It was stifling hot in the valley, though the approaching storm was shipping winds enough to rock my easel. Thunder crashed and rumbled in the distant mountain ranges while the sky took on darker grey by degrees.

I had to paint quickly to capture the emotion of the changing, advancing thunderstorm. The hot winds and ominous sky imparted vitality that I'd lost in the hubbub of town.

June 29

Eleven years ago today, in one state below Oregon, my father died. The cessation of his life brought me new life. If he would have lived, most likely my mother would have also. Then I would have had parents to guide me, help me, and most likely interfere with my growing. If I would have had parents, I might not have as much of myself as I have now. I wouldn't have built my own home in the mountains and this little niche I've carved here.

If I would have had parents, life might not have been such a struggle. I would feel secure having someone to fall back on, a home to go to when I was homeless, a sense of belonging. Instead, I've had to find all of this within me, and sometimes when I'm tired and lonely I forget that I have it all within me.

I am glad that when my parents died I was feeling such love for them. They will always remain in my mind and heart as the best, perfect parents. They gave me their all. I miss them both and wish they could see all that I've done on my own. I know they would be proud of me for all that I am, just as I admired them for all that they were.

When I hear people talk negatively about their parents I get so angry, and want to lash out and tell them they don't know how lucky they are to always have love and something to fall back on when the going gets hard. I want to tell these children, grown now, no longer dependent on their parents as small children are, to grow a bit further and be thankful for their parents.

June 30

It is ardent and persistent determination that keeps me going up here. And it is caution, always keeping five steps ahead of myself, that keeps me alive.

It hasn't been easy. If I thought/felt building this cabin three years ago with help was hard then, hard has a more potent definition now that I've taken to building this log cabin alone. The philosophy behind this cabin is: build it small enough, with small enough logs, so that I can build it alone. But these logs have shot the hell out of my theory. With an average diameter of ten inches and a weight somewhere between three and four hundred pounds apiece, my 105 pounds of bone, flesh and muscle ain't enough to easily maneuver one of these logs.

I spent four hours today wrestling two logs with butts of 13 inches—porch joists—up onto the foundation walls. I tried lifting one end up and wrestling it onto the wall, then lifting up the other end. I grunted and quivered under the log's weight and wished I had dedicated myself prior to this work to working out in the weight room. Between rolling, lifting and shoving, pivoting their weight with mine, I got two logs up and rebarred down. Tomorrow I begin to notch.

The pain in my lower back tonight is intense. The muscles are still tied up in the afternoon's effort.

July 3

The bear is teaching me about fear. Fear is what I want it to be, rational or irrational. The bear is rational fear. The bear is real. Rational fear is dealing with real fright, tangible, visible. Irrational fear cannot be seen or touched, it is in the mind, imagined.

I did not imagine the snorts and bangs filtering up between the floor boards. Even banging on the garbage can and shooting out the window did not scare away the bear last night. I tried barring the door, but any material I could use was outside on the porch. Not possessing the courage to step outside, I was forced to secure my fortress with a can opener. I nailed one end to the door, the other end into the door jamb. I used what lay in my means to protect me from what lay beyond my means. I had used everything in my power to protect me from the bear—a fire poker, can opener, trash can, a gun. If the bear was going to break in, there was nothing more I could do. I had to accept the fear, let go of any irrational emotions and face the reality of this frightening predicament.

If I let my imagination take me into the bear's jaws, between its paws, my fear increased. If I focused on my reality, that I was safe inside the cabin, the bear was outside and would not or could not possibly climb up into the loft, then I was not afraid. Fear can be idealistic, conceived, invented, envisioned, but it is not real fear. This is where I can get into trouble, if I let my imagination develop fear.

As if to verify my inner philosophy, an omen flew into the window last night as I lay in bed, thinking. A dark creature flapped into the open dormer window. An electric fright snapped me rigid. A slight glow surrounded its thrashing wings. As soon as I had made out the creature as a flying thing and accepted the consequence of its presence in my life, my fear left, and so did the creature—out the window.

I knew then that the creature was a teacher, come in to instruct me in the ways of fear. I felt then I could tolerate the bear and turn terror into acceptance. I woke many times last night, waiting for the creature to come back. It didn't. Only the light from a sliver of the moon flashed through my window.

July 11

Living alone here and doing what I am doing is an infinite source of struggle. But coping with the struggles teaches me a greater sense of self-strength, an inner awareness, than I can think of receiving from any other person or thing. I can think of no other experience than building alone with logs where I have felt such a burst of accomplishment and confidence, even though some days my efforts have achieved very little.

There is another part of me that lives strongly here. The painter in me, the poet, that merges with moonrises, sunsets, creeks rushing white over mossy granite. When painting, I feel so immense, want to dance with exhilaration, the speck that I am on the landscape. These past two nights I have painted the moon in meadows, forests and valleys. I have watched her arch across the sky, felt her mystical pull. It is times like that that can erase all the sorrowful moments of living alone here, because it is moments like these that I live for.

July 12

The moon gave to me last night, after I took time to give to it. Late in the night when my mind should have been sleeping, it took me, along with my sleeping bag and my rifle, down to the meadow where I took up my vigil. I lay in my sleeping bag, a dot in the open expanse of grass, under the moon-dome. I could see the partially highlighted valley, and upward into the silhouetted mountains. I sketched the different perspectives, having to use my flashlight, because pen scratches are more exacting than paint patches. I wanted to first sketch the exactness of the scenes before me, then images from inside of me.

I saw the ribbing of my blue down bag run counter to the concentric light rings of the moon. I felt my belly fill with light and float like a blimp towards the moon-pull. I felt like I was in a cathedral of heavenly light.

Thunder clouds rumbled, parted their veil from the moon, who shot light across the grass and pine-covered land. Rain from passing clouds wet my protruding head. I didn't mind; the moisture and cold on my face, my warm body wrapped in feathery cocoon, and moonlight, were entertaining sensations.

George Gammow's words kept resonating in my thoughts. So, the moon is the daughter of the earth's surface. A cast-off of hot gas, separated during the course of extended revolutions from that part of earth's face now marked as the Pacific Ocean, and thrown into the galaxy almost 240,000 miles away. Suddenly I made a connection.

There is a spot of ocean below a certain bluff I am drawn to in Mendocino. This spot of ocean is surrounded by jets of jagged cliff. I can remember standing there last year and for no reason, I thought, "This is where the moon was born."

In the mountain meadow, now, the moon did not seem thousands of miles distant. She was an extension of me, a beating force like my heart. Her revolutions revolved in me, her light was my iris, changing as clouds floated across her face. I gazed on the moon until it dropped behind the mountains, and then slept.

Later in the night I was awakened by the constant splatter of rain. Groggy, and with a bellyache, I stuffed my bag and walked up the mountain, beginning again to fear the night. Tree stumps transformed into bears and bobcats. Any rustling was some animal charging through the woods to devour me. I started chanting a few words about keeping my mind clear, contained and fearless. I slept in my bed that night, the storm releasing, outside, a spring of Indian paint over my heart.

To my surprise, as I walked to the creek for my morning splash, blood streamed down my leg. Early! I'm never early. What did Gammow say? Something about the forces of lunar attraction being stronger on the side of the earth turned towards the moon. Gravitational pull causes tides to oscillate, planets to revolve, seasons to change, and blood to flow from female gonads.

July 13

Awake at 3:45, and by 4:15 observe the subtle ranges of red, constantly changing and poking hot holes through a once-dark forest. By 4:30 I've come to understand why my last painting of the sunrise phenomenon didn't work. I did not make a delicate enough transition between the intense tangerine of the sky and the spaces between the forest foliage.

The light between the trees is not just orange, but a mixture of cadmium yellow, red, and white, before it takes a later turn up into a cobalt blue day sky. The light between the trees is not just light, but energy.

July 14

I am beginning to feel very solid in my aloneness here. Going to town once a week affords me enough human contact to feed me through the next week. I am learning to unfold my energies throughout the day in order to accomplish what I have set out to accomplish.

My body still aches, especially my lower back from the lifting, but it is healthy pain. Progress is slow. I have only been getting about two logs up in a five-hour work day.

After I finally lift a log up onto the wall, I have to line it up with the one below, dog it down, scribe out the notch, roll it over, dog the log down again, climb down the wall and start the saw, then climb back up and saw out my marks before I can whack out the wedges with my Collins axe, then finish the notch with the curved adze. Sometimes it takes me six tries of rolling and re-rolling the log into place before I can get it to fit snugly on the bottom log. It is getting more dangerous to work alone now that the walls are gaining some height. I have to start the saw on the ground, then climb back up on the wall and pull it back up to me on a rope. Sometimes the saw dies out in mid-air, and I have to climb back down and do it all over again. Then there is the balancing act I must perform in order to straddle the logs.

Despite the pains, frustrations, and initial "Woe is me!" I have been doing it alone and liking the work. Building this cabin alone, rather than with men as I did on the cabin I live in now, is 100% more difficult but also 100% more fulfilling. I don't have to put up with all the tool grabbing, the "Here, let me do it," like I did before. Working on this cabin alone is like a test of everything I learned the first time around. I give myself time to learn from my mistakes. I push myself beyond those points where I think I can push no more.

July 22

Work on the cabin is becoming more difficult each day. Since the walls have gotten so high I cannot safely position a log up on the top to notch down. If I am lucky, I can finagle a visitor into helping me lift a couple of logs up there—which I can notch down later. When the work becomes as difficult as it has been, it becomes a supreme effort to get myself down to the building site to work. I usually work in the hottest part of the day, which really saps my energy, but I love the pounding hot sun on my body. I love the sweat and the filth. Then I plunge into the creek and revive myself, renew myself, and feel like a wild animal. I fall into bed at night with a full and healthy fatigue.

July 23

At times what I paint is not necessarily meant to result in anything familiar. The end product is the process of finding symbology reflective of my evolution in a primal manner that enables me to experience nature. I am, through painting, able to become aware of the supernatural truths that lie beyond the forms I paint.

August 6

Tonight the moon parts storm clouds. It makes itself

known by highlighting the hillside across the creek.

This cabin is a mess. I've been chiseling boards to fit the walls to make a new set of shelves. There are books and papers all over. Yuck! What a pig-pen. But I get a great satisfaction out of my mess. I am a jackass of all trades, mistress of the moon.

I took a four-mile hike down Fern Creek this afternoon. On the last leg homeward, pushing through some bushes, I came across a porcupine. It raised its back and all the quills stood up.

August 15

I celebrate the last round of wall logs, laid up and notched down, by indulging in a good bottle of wine; not wine from a jug, but a bottle that needs to be uncorked.

The studio looks like a log box. It stands about 18 feet high from the foundation to the last loft log. The first floor is about eight feet tall, with the loft walls raised another five feet, and the foundation making up the rest. It's hard to believe that something so simple looking could have taxed me so heavily. I'm not even going to attempt to begin raising rafters or laying the floor. What is left of my summer—two weeks—will be spent using time in the way time is not allowed once I return to Mendocino; being a wild child.

Building the studio has taken two summers already. By the end of next summer I should be ready to paint there. I know I'll need help with the roof, maybe the main floor, and putting in the windows and skylights. Three summers, taken up to realize I am both less and more than I think I am.

In the Deep Heart's Core

Becky Birtha

I

Those places up the coast had wonderful names. Point Reyes. Mendocino. Inverness. That last one always made Sahara think of the place in the Yeats poem, The Lake Isle of Innisfree:

I will arise and go now, and go to Innisfree.

Sahara came to this part of the country for the first time when she first struck out on her own. Twenty years have passed since then, and now she has returned. She has come back to a particular place, this time. But that first time, twenty years ago, she traveled up and down this road for no better reason than that she liked the sound of the names.

At the end of one of those long ago days, she had

stood by a roadside, hitchhiking. She'd had no luck the past half hour, and had walked maybe two or three miles already along the road, turning to stretch her arm out straight every time a car passed. There was gritty sand in her socks. Sand had worked its way under her kerchief and settled in her scalp, among the thick, coarse crinkles of her hair. Sand clung beneath her nails and lined the pockets of the faded smock she wore over her patched up blue jeans. She stood with her feet planted far apart, and was glad of her big-boned frame, taking up its space, glad of her height—her size letting them know she could take care of herself. Being outdoors all summer long had bronzed her face from tan to copper brown, and she was glad of it, the earth color distinct to everyone who passed, glad of who she was.

Night was coming. The sun slanted red, sinking over the ocean side of the road. Watching it, she had seen the foot path that led off down the bank. She had crossed the road and followed it. She didn't know that there was another way in, a steep rutted drive a little ways up the highway. She had been surprised to find the space the path led her to scattered with colorful cars and vans.

Where she found herself was not on the beach she had expected, but on an enormous wide plateau, a grassy place that was open and expansive, yet sheltered and hidden. It was walled on one side by the sandy banks that led up to the road. She had walked through the long grass, across to the other edge of the open field, and found that the land ended abruptly in a sudden drop down a sheer cliff to the sounding ocean hundreds of yards below. She stood at the edge; the wind whipped through her, and she could see far out to sea. Later, someone told her it was as far west as you could go. The Headlands, she found out they called it.

It was a place where people gathered—folk traveling up and down the coast. Some of them were on holiday—summer gypsies who'd return to some snug town place in a week or a month. Others, in ancient khaki garb and rundown boots, looked as though they had been on the road all their lives. And there were a few who, like Sahara, seemed to be just finding a place from which to begin. They had come in beat-up cars or housecars—pickup trucks with handmade houses perched on their beds—in battered, rusted-out vans and panel trucks, or brightly painted ones. Some, like her, had come walking or hitchhiking, everything they still cared about owning on their backs. They would stay a night, a week, make friends, make love, make decisions about their lives, move on.

Now, twenty years later, Sahara is one of those who has driven here—in a battered blue van. She is not sure why she is back on the road. Or for how long. She did not give notice at the school where she has worked for the past five years. But when she closed up her classroom in June, packing the supplies away, scrubbing the chairs and cots, taking down the posters and bulletin boards, she felt that it was the last time. She couldn't keep on, year after year, loving a whole new class of children, then letting them go.

When she set out in her van at the start of this summer, it seemed there was something drawing her back to this place she had found quite by accident so long ago. It seemed there was something calling her here, some voice that did not stop. Was it the ocean, sounding night and day against the cliffs down below the Headlands, the ocean calling to her? She doesn't know—only knows that if she stays, time will tell why she has come back.

She has been here for three nights and three days now, and has found that twenty years have not changed the place much. Traveling people have not forgotten it. At night someone will build a fire and people will share whatever they have. It is nearly night now. Sahara has taken the largest pot, and gone across the road for water.

Down the road, she first sees the girl, standing where a car has just left her off. The girl faces the traffic that doesn't come, her boots planted far apart. The sun is in her eyes, but she doesn't shade them, and she doesn't take the pack off her back and let it down to rest in the sand by the side of the road. She hasn't a sign with a destination on it. But she does have a map—draws it out of her back pocket and opens it out. She turns to look back up the road and then moves her finger across the map. She folds it to a different square, studies it a little longer, and shoves it into the back pocket of the brown corduroys.

A moment later, she notices the path sloping down the bank between the scrubby bushes, just across the road. Sahara watches the way she hitches up the pack a bit, then looks up and down the road. And Sahara knows the girl is imagining a soft beach to sleep on tonight, high above the level of the tide, just as Sahara did when she first came to this place, very young, on foot, and alone.

Sahara would have been called a girl then, too. Now there is ash gray in the short hair that is tied up beneath her fringed kerchief. Under the spigot, the water splashes over a network of tiny wrinkles on her hands. And when she lifts the pot, the veins stand out on the back of her hand and arm. Her skirt sweeps the grasses as she follows, in long, even strides, down the path where the girl disappeared.

Already, there is a ring of faces around the firelight. Whatever they have brought, they will share. Some nights there is little. Wild peas someone has gathered along the road, thrown into the stew. Abalone or a little fish. Wild berries. Other nights, people stopping have brought food, and there is plenty.

This is one of the nights of plenty. There's meat, and someone has brought fresh sourdough bread.

Two long-haired children tag each other in and out of the firelight, until the smell from the big pot finally draws them in and settles them still.

The girl from the roadside has found her way to the gathering and is standing at the back of the circle. Someone calls out to her, "Come on over by the fire. Pull up a chair."

The girl shows a brief flicker of a smile, and moves in next to Sahara. The sudden closeness of her changes something in the air, draws Sahara to an alertness, an awareness that feels like wakefulness of a part of her that has been asleep. She feels, too, as if she's wise to something the girl doesn't yet know—having watched her on the road, maybe. She feels there is a reason the girl has chosen her, out of the circle, to sit beside—some reason the girl herself is not conscious of. She turns to speak. The girl's eyes are wary.

"I'm Sahara," Sahara says. And then, "If you've got a cup or a bowl or something, you might want to get it out."

A big woman in overalls with a blue star tattooed on her arm is ladling out the stew. She holds up a wooden bowl and someone says, "Over here," and the bowl is passed that way. When she gets to the girl's blue and white enameled cup, someone says, "It's his," jerking a thumb over beside Sahara.

The girl shakes the hair out of her eyes and reaches to take the cup. "Hers," she says with half a smile on her lips. But she says it so softly that only Sahara hears it.

To Sahara, it's clear that the girl is a womanchild, nearly a woman. It would have been, even in this gathering darkness, even if Sahara had not seen her on the road. Perhaps her clothes are deceiving. Besides the boots and corduroys, she is wearing a denim jacket with the sleeves cut off. There is nothing on her arms, and there seems to be nothing beneath the jacket. She hasn't any breasts.

But her face is a woman's face. The brown eyes are wide and uncertain, and her mouth, even just smiling halfway, changes the whole look into something so far from harshness you know she is somebody's daughter. Beneath the locks of short brown hair, Sahara can see tiny drops of silver in her earlobes. The girl's skin is tanned. Her face makes Sahara think of a locket—a heart-shaped locket shut tight on a secret.

She knows she has never seen this person before, and yet she can feel herself straining to place her, to figure out who she is. She watches the girl, and the girl watches silently while the others talk.

"I'm thinking about going up around the Russian River, see if there's any work in the lumber business."

"I don't know. Up in Oregon, where I come from, people been laid off that worked there thirty years."

A baby wakes and starts to cry. A woman reaches to take it from its father, holds it in the crook of her arm and lifts up her sweater on one side.

Sahara looks away. It hurts her to watch that—something she will never have now.

"Brought the whole family this time, huh?" Someone says to the father with a grin.

"Oh, yeah. Even brought the kitchen sink. We live in that yellow pickup over there. That little fella's never lived in a house, and I hope he never will."

Sahara watches the girl next to her as her eyes follow the man's finger, over to the cabin that is perched on the back of the pickup, with its gabled roof and stained glass windows and domed skylight. The girl's eyes widen, and she keeps on looking at it for a long time.

The talk eddies and swirls around them. The fire burns lower. Some people depart for the café in the town, a few miles away. And the children are put to bed. The girl's backpack would make a fine backrest or pillow, but she sits bolt upright, with her back straight. Her legs are crossed, and every part of her is stiffly still. Only her fingers never stop moving, itching, twisting around one another, clasping and unclasping, opening and closing. She stares into the fire. The firelight flickers and leaps in her womanchild's face, in her wide eyes.

Sahara knows she must be the one to begin. In her low voice, she phrases one of the two age-old questions of the road. "Where you from?"

The girl startles from the trance of the fire, and turns to look at her. In the moment that it takes, Sahara imagines herself as this girl must see her. Old. To someone as young as her, Sahara's near forty years will seem much older than they seem to Sahara. The girl won't see the gray that salts her hair. It's covered with the bright gold kerchief, tied like an Arab headdress, hanging down her neck and back. But even in the firelight, she'll see the lines in Sahara's face, the crow's-feet at the corners of her eyes, and likely the hairs on her chin. She will see old. And black. An old black woman in dowdy clothes from a secondhand store, with a gaudy headrag wrapped around her head. She won't see who Sahara really is.

The girl has turned back to stare at the fire, after answering the question with just one word. "Oakland."

Sahara watches her a minute more. It is the girl's fingers that won't be still in her lap, that finally make her go on and ask the other question.

"Where you headed?"

She sighs a long sigh, and says, "Just traveling." But she draws up one knee to lean against and turns to Sahara.

"Me, too," Sahara says, smiling. "Just traveling, this time. You been on the road long?"

The girl shakes her head from side to side. "I just left home. This morning."

"No kidding? This morning? For the first time?"

"Yeah. Well, I ran away a couple of times before. But I was just a kid. This is different. This time I won't go back there. Ever!"

"What happened?" As soon as she's said it, she knows it's wrong. And the girl, who'd turned to face her, now jerks her gaze away, back to the fire.

"It was just time for me to leave, that's all. It wasn't really my home anyway. It was my grandparents' place. And it was time for me to get out, that's all." Now she has drawn up the other knee, her arms wrapped tight around, so that her shape is a hard, stiff triangle.

"I guess that time comes for everybody," Sahara says. "Everybody who's ever going to be her own person." She stares into the fire, remembering how it was. "I left home when I was eighteen. My mother thought the world of me, and tried to give me everything, but it wasn't enough for me. I had to have something of my own." She had always meant to go back and set things right with her mother, years later when she would be an equal, married, with children of her own, when the things they had quarreled over wouldn't matter any more. She'd always thought there'd be plenty of time for that and then, one summer, when Sahara was halfway around the world, her mother had suddenly died....

"I went on the road, too," she tells the girl beside her. "That was all I wanted to do. Hitchhike cross-country. Get out to California. Didn't know the first thing about how to do it. I mean, I didn't even know how to read a road map right to get out of my home town. First time a tractor trailer ever stopped for me, I didn't know how to climb up there. I didn't know some pretty basic safety stuff I ought to've known either. Like to check the locks on the doors of the car before you get in, make sure you can get out." She's eyeing the girl's profile, hoping she's listening, wishing she'd ask what else. There's so much Sahara knows now that would have made things easier, if someone had told her. "Or even," she says, "to always go to a woman if you get in trouble and need some kind of help. Don't ever depend on a man." She waits, but the girl doesn't answer, doesn't ask. And Sahara knows how scared she is.

People are returning from the town. Somewhere, someone picks up a guitar, and a quiet song spills out of the nearby darkness. Sahara stands; her skirt falls in billows to the ground. She stretches, reaching her hands out for one last feel of the fire's warmth, then moves away, to do the things she needs to do for the night.

She collects her sleeping bag from the battered blue van and comes back by way of the fire, crouching for a second beside the girl. "You got a sleeping bag? Or blankets or anything?"

"Huh? Oh, yeah. A sleeping bag."

"It's a good night for sleeping out," Sahara says. "I've got an old van here, but I only use it when it rains." She nods her head over toward the far side of this grassy place, away from the road. "I always like to sleep out there, on the Headlands. In the morning when you wake up, you can look right out over the ocean."

"I think I'll just stay here awhile longer," the girl says.

"Got a lot on your mind to think about, huh?"

"Yeah," she says. "Yeah, I guess so."

"Well, if it helps your thinking any to talk, come over and talk to me. I'll be awake a bit longer. And I wake up easy, too. I don't mind—if something's troubling you." She smiles at the girl, trying to let her know that she wants to be a friend.

"Thanks," the girl says. And smiles back—a self-conscious smile, but a whole one, this time. It makes Sahara feel as if a door has suddenly swung wide open in this night, a door into a bright, new place that has never been entered.

The wind is high, blowing shreds and shards of gray clouds across a three-quarter moon. Sahara places her sleeping bag with the head facing the bluffs. She turns her shoes upside down and makes a pillow, under the sleeping bag, of the sweater she has taken off. Then she lies still in her bag, on her back, and lets the memories come flooding in. It is the children that she is always remembering, all the children who have passed through her life.

II

The first time Sahara went to sleep in a house where she was alone with children, she had a hard time sleeping. In her head she went over in detail the whole layout of the house, with its abundance of doors and halls and private baths. She did not know it as well as she should, and wondered if she could really find her way if there were a fire and she was half asleep.

The Weatherbys had not bothered to question how she might deal with emergencies, or even ask what her experience had been. They had looked at her and not seen a teenager who had never done anything like this before. They had seen, in her dark face and her tall, womanly frame, only generations of cooks and "help," nursemaids and nannies.... The interview with Mrs. Weatherby hadn't even taken fifteen minutes. The woman was so overjoyed at finding someone on such short notice, so relieved that she would not have to cancel the week in the Bahamas after all, that she had explained all this in much greater detail than she explained about Heather's temper tantrums or Bradley's asthma.

In the stuffy little spare room, Sahara worried until she couldn't keep her eyes open any longer. Three hours later she was wide awake, as though a voice had called her. Down the long hall, there was only silence, but she threw on her robe and padded in her bare feet to the rooms where the children slept.

Peter Weatherby was hunched in the middle of his bed with the covers pulled over his head. He was crying. Sahara sat by his side and rubbed his back in wide, slow circles. She did not want to talk or sing, afraid she might wake the others. So, very softly, she recited poems to him—"The Owl and the Pussycat," "Wynken, Blynken and Nod," "Little Brown Baby"—all the ones that her own mother had read to her, over and over again. Her hand kept stroking the warm dampness of his soft pajamas, circling in the rhythm of the verses—until he slept.

Still she sat there, a long time after, watching the mound of his small body rise and fall in gentle regularity. He had cried. And she, at the other end of the hall, the other end of the house, had not heard, but had known. He had cried and she had put him back to sleep. It was as if she had passed through some ritual, some initiation....

*

In the night, there are only quiet noises, the ocean at the foot of the cliffs, and the dry grasses rustling. The wind is restless still, whirrs in Sahara's ears and washes her bare face cold and clean. Overhead, most of the clouds have blown off and stars are out.

The ancient rhyme comes into her head. "Starlight, starbright, first star I see tonight...." She has always made the same wish, over and over, on every star and wishbone, every milkweed seed caught and dandelion blown away, on all the birthday candles. Whenever she heard the words "heart's desire," she thought of a child.

She never wanted a man. And she chose a way of life—without men—in which children did not easily appear. Sometimes it seems she has spent her whole life finding ways to get close to other people's children.

*

The child who did not know how to play was a little girl, a Puertorriqueña. Her name was Elizabeth Maldonado. She was three. Elizabeth's mother came into Sahara's classroom holding her small daughter's hand and gazed around the colorful playroom. She spoke to Sahara in a voice barely loud enough to hear. "*Mi hija, mi Elizabeth—no sabe jugar.* She is not like my other children. She does not play. *Es la única cosa*—that is the one thing I care about ... maybe ... you can teach her?"

In the playroom the children clustered around the sandbox that stood on tall legs by the window. They patted up mountains and highways, scooped out tunnels and lakes. Their high-pitched voices bargained and traded, cried for a turn with the dump truck, shrieked with delight.

Elizabeth stood in the center of the room, a crumpled tissue in one hand, a tiny doll house figure in the other. Her slender body swaying in the short cotton dress, she rocked rhythmically heels to toes, toes to heels. There was a whisper of a smile on her face; her eyes were far away.

When Sahara got closer, she could hear her humming—a toneless tune that never began or ended, just went on and on. Sahara stooped to the little girl's level and lightly put an arm around her shoulders, smiling into her eyes. "What's that you have in your hand, Elizabeth? *¿Qué tienes en la mano? Ah—una muñeca.* Can you say that? *Muñeca. ¿Es tuyo?*"

On the playground those first weeks of fall, the other children would come tumbling over to her, short brown and tan and pale legs pumping, untied sneakers and soft plastic sandals pounding across the asphalt. "Teacher!" "*¡Maestra!*" "Miss Sahara!" "Elizabeth doesn't want a turn to ride." "Can I have Elizabeth's turn, Miss Sahara? Please?"

"Oh, no. Elizabeth *needs* her turn. Where is she? *Vente,* Elizabeth. *Ven acá.*" Taking her by the hand, she led her to the tricycle, while the little girl lagged back and shook her head. "Come on go for a ride. We'll go slow—*muy suave.*"

Come, Elizabeth. I'll climb the sliding board with you. I'll touch the sticky paste first. We'll pat the rabbit together....

In January, Franklin crossed the playroom, his chestnut round face more pleased than angry. "Hey, you know what, Miss Sahara? Elizabeth talked to me. She said, 'You go away!' "

Another day, Manuela came crying. "Elizabeth took the baby's bottle. I had it first." In the playhouse corner, Sahara could see Elizabeth, tangly brown hair curtaining her face, slight figure bent over the carriage, holding the plastic nursing bottle to the baby doll's mouth.

There was an afternoon on the playground again, nearly the last week of school, and the end of the day. Across the street she could see Mrs. Hughes waiting for the light to change, and Franklin had seen her too, was already collecting his paintings and the wooden airplane he had made. Down the block, Mrs. Maldonado came pushing the baby's stroller in front of her.

Sahara looked around for Elizabeth. The little girl was just starting up the ladder of the sliding board. She was always very serious about this, hands clamping the railings, patent leather pumps stepping one rung at a time, her small chin set with determination. Sahara stopped her for a second with her hand on the child's back. "When you get up to the top, look and see who's coming."

The child reached the summit. She stood between the high arched railings, a hand on each one, and scanned the horizon. And her tiny face broke into a furious grin. "*¡Mami! ¡Mami! ¡Mira, Mami!*"

She swept down the shining length of the slide, landing on her feet and ran, brown hair flying, ran laughing across the entire playground, out the open gate, and into her mother's arms.

*

Sahara will never forget the image of that little girl, arms open, laughing and running—away from her. She will not forget any of them, though years have passed, and they are scattered in different cities all across the country.

Quiet nights in open places, the boundaries are unguarded, and they come back to her. Peter and Elizabeth and so many others. Like joy. .

*

Sahara lived with Joy, Joy's mother Janet, four other women and two other children in a big sprawling old house in the heart of the city, maybe ten years ago, now. Joy was another child who couldn't play. Tamika and Nicholas would be racing up and down the stairs after school, calling out to each other and shouting. "I can't find my skate key!" "Hey, will you hold the door while I get my bike out?" "Wait up! Wait for me!"

Joy's delicate dark fingers closed only with straining effort around a crayon or pencil, and the pictures came out a snarl of faintly marked scribbles. Bikes and skates, even scissors and puzzles were impossible.

Tamika and Nicholas ran in and out—for a piece of chalk, a glass of water—the door screen banging behind them. Sahara sat on the couch with Joy in her lap, the soft pile of Joy's short hair against her cheek, and read picture book after picture book. "And when he came to the place where the wild things are they roared their terrible roars...."

"And gna-a-ashed their ter-ri-ble tee-e-eeth...," Joy's small voice drawled, forcing out the syllables one by one with effort. The words came out distorted, but she had them all memorized. After living with her for a month, Sahara could understand almost everything Joy said. It was like listening to words slowed down on a tape recorder that she could speed up in her head. Or like learning to decipher someone's handwriting. "And ro-o-olled their terri-ble eye-s...."

"And showed their terrible claws." Outside, she could hear Tamika and her girlfriends.

"That ain't the way you draw a hopscotch, girl. Onesies posed to be all by itself." "I'm first, when she get finished." "Nu-uh! I already said it."

Tamika and Nicholas were only a year and two years older than Joy. But they didn't play with her. Sahara had heard one of Tamika's friends asking once, just outside the window, "How come your sister still has to be in a stroller?" And Tamika declaring hotly, "That's not my sister!"

Nicholas and Tamika had quickly made friends with each other and made their own friends in the neighborhood. Their friends lived with mothers and fathers, or mothers and brothers and sisters, or even with grandmothers, but not with multi-ethnic collections of odd assorted women who weren't related to them or to each other. Their friends were never invited in, by either Tamika or Nicholas.

"... And into the night of his very own room where he found his supper waiting for him and it was still hot." She closed *Where the Wild Things Are* and slapped it down on the pile on the floor below them, spilled Joy onto the couch and stood up. "That's it. I'm not reading any more stories. Know what we're gonna do now?"

"Wha-a-at?"

"We're gonna sail away. To where the wild things are."

A table turned upside down was their boat, the broom and mop were oars. Joy steadied the sail and kept a sharp look out for islands on the horizon. Sahara rowed and sang "Heave Away Santyanna" and "The Sloop John B." They caught fish with one of Joy's long shoelaces. And then Joy dropped the sail, her palms patting the upturned underside of the table beneath her. Her eyes were pools of dismay. "O-oh no-o."

"What is it? What's the matter?" Sahara was instantly alert, the play forgotten.

"It's we-et."

Sahara began to pat the floor too, feeling anxiously around Joy's bottom. Everything was absolutely dry. Joy heaved out a guffaw of laughter at Sahara's antics and finished triumphantly, "I think we sss-pru-ung a lee-e-eak."

They were busy bailing out when Nicholas came in, and didn't notice him until he walked through the ocean and right up to the side of the boat and said, "Hey what are you doing? How come you turned over the table?"

"This isn't a table," Sahara corrected.

Joy grinned and said, "If you do-on't sstart sss-wimming you're go-ing to dro-o-own."

"Can I play?" Nicholas asked.

Sahara nearly answered, but Joy cut her off. "I kno-o-ow." Her voice was loud and sure. "He can be one of the wi-i-ild things."

*

Whatever became of them? Joy would be fifteen or sixteen now, Nicholas maybe eighteen. But the house had broken up at the end of the first year. Eventually, she had lost touch with all of them.

When Sahara sleeps, she dreams of children. Babies and children—they come to her in dreams every night. Each is distinct and different from any other. Each has her own voice, his own shape, her own face like no one else in the world.

III

Something has awakened her on this night, just as it

did on that first night long ago, knowing that one of the children was awake, and in trouble.

She listens. The wind has died as it always does, along toward morning. The night is absolutely still. Only the tops of the grasses rustle softly. Above her, the clouds have all blown off; the vast blackness is alight with stars, the milky way cutting a wide swath across the center. The girl has brought her sleeping bag and stretched it out on the ground along next to Sahara's.

Sahara sits up and studies the figure beside her. There's a scent of dye and fresh fabric from the sleeping bag—it must have been bought new for this adventure. Its inhabitant lies still, with her face turned away and half covered. Sahara knows she is crying.

She hesitates, torn over whether to allow the girl her space, or to enter it. Where does she belong in this person's life? Does she belong at all? Finally she reaches out and rests a hand for a moment on the girl's shoulder through the thick, quilted material. "I'm awake," she says, "if you want to talk about it."

The girl doesn't answer at first. Then her voice comes out, scratchy with tears. "That won't help."

"Maybe not. Maybe it won't change anything. But if you tell someone, then at least you don't have to carry it all by yourself." She waits a moment, then goes on. "You know, that's one of the things I found out is so special about the road—it keeps your secrets for you. You can talk to somebody you just met and tell them anything. After tonight you never have to see me again." She waits a bit longer, then asks, "What happened?"

"Nothing," the girl says.

"I mean back at home—*something* happened."

"I just had to get out of there, that's all. It wasn't my

home, anyway. They never let me forget *that.*"

"Did they ... did your grandparents throw you out?"

The girl has squirmed to sit up, wiping her face with the heels of her hands. Now she laughs a laugh that is like a handful of stones thrown down on concrete. "I told him not to bother. The bastard. I told him not to waste his breath. Said I was capable of walking out that door without any help from him. And I did it, too."

"Something he did made you furious...."

"Everything he did drove me crazy! He's always so smug and proud of himself—he can't ever let me forget it for a minute how they took me in and raised me. I'm supposed to be humble and grateful for the rest of my life." She let another pebble of hard laughter fall. "That's not giving.

"Every time I do anything he doesn't like, any little thing, he goes crazy. He said I was going to end up just like her." She turns suddenly, to seek out Sahara's face in the darkness. "My mother, I mean. I'm gonna end up another disgrace to the family. Ashamed to come home." Her eyes hold Sahara's in the quiet, charcoal darkness. "He calls her a slut. Right to my face. He says that about my mother! He says I'm gonna end up a slut just like her."

She looks away again, out into the night. Her hands have begun to play with the edge of the quilted fabric, pleating it into harried ruffles, letting it go, taking it up again. "I didn't even do anything. He won't ever give me a chance to explain. Him and his dirty mind. Just because I was out all night he thinks I was screwing around. I wasn't even with a boy. I was with Marianne Delarosa. Just cause I like to talk to her. We were up talking all night, sitting in her brother's truck."

She is silent for a few moments, looking out over the

distance, out over the Headlands where, far below, the voice of the ocean is suddenly loud, sounding against the rocky wall of the cliff. For a moment, everything about the girl is still; even her fingers lie resting.

"Everybody says my mother ran off with another woman. Some woman she met over in the city that nobody knew. But they won't ever tell me any more than that. They act like it's something I'm not supposed to know. My grandparents won't talk about it at all. Except to point out how I'm turning out just like her." Her fingers close on a clump of grass beside her and rip the long blades from the ground, tearing them into bits. "So what if I *am* like her? I'm *supposed* to be like her. She was my mother! She got out of there when she was eighteen and I swore to God I would, too."

"That must have hurt you a lot," Sahara says softly. The locket face turns to her; the girl looks surprised that Sahara is still there. "The way she left you there, I mean," Sahara says. "That she got out herself, but she didn't take you—she left you there."

The girl is brushing sudden fresh tears back from the sides of her face with the heels of her hands. "It doesn't matter," she says. "Because I got out now, too. And I'm going to find her."

"Your mother?"

"Yeah. That's really why I left—and where I'm going."

"So she stayed in touch with you?"

"Well, not exactly. We haven't been in touch. But I know she was supposed to have gone up north. Headed for Vancouver. That's what everybody said."

Sahara looks over to check her face, but the girl is completely serious. She's leaning on one elbow now, her look full of that confidence in herself that doesn't last long past eighteen. "Vancouver's a big place," Sahara says softly.

The girl seems not to have heard. "And I know what she looks like. Everybody says I look just like her."

"Of course," Sahara says gently, "she'd be older now."

"Of course," the girl answers, lightly.

"And she must have lived through a lot. I mean, she may not be the person you think she is...."

"Then I want to know who she is, now. I want her to know who *I* am."

And Sahara thinks, no *you* want to know who you are. You want her to give you that. And she never will, even if you find her. No one can.

"Whoever she is," the girl says, "I don't care. She's my mother. I'm going to find her. I don't care if it takes me the rest of my life."

Now the girl is lying back, with her arms folded under her head, watching the sky. "Sure are a lot of stars out here," she says, and her voice sounds hushed and small against the vast night.

Sahara slips down in her bag and turns on her back to view them, too. "Sure are. It's funny to think how, down here, they all look close together and pretty much the same. But up there every one is different, and they're millions of miles apart." She wants to go on: You might as well go wandering off into the sky, little girl, and try to find just one star.

"You know, your mother could be anywhere," she says, finally. "She could be camping out right here on this roadside tonight."

"I never thought of that. I guess she could." The girl turns that one over in her mind, and says, doubtfully, "Maybe I should stay here for awhile." Then she asks, "Are *you* going to be staying here long?"

"I don't know. I could stay a while longer." She's thinking, thinking about what happens next, in her life. She listens to the sound of the waves, striking on the rock below, striking and splashing, roaring and repeating. Something like that never-ending sound has called her back here, after all these years, to this place to begin from, begin again.

Twenty years ago, that first time, she sat looking out over these same cliffs another bright, starry night, and a woman sat beside her who seemed old to Sahara then. She was the one who told Sahara what this place was. She said, "Where we're sitting now is as far west as you can go. This cape is the end of the land, and these Headlands are the end of the cape. Everybody always wants to travel west, but when you get here you have to change directions."

Sahara lifts up a little to look over at the girl who lies watching the stars. "I might be going north in another few days," she tells her. "It's been a long time since I've been in Vancouver."

There's some kind of softness, a warmth, that has come stealing up in the windless dark and circled the two of them all the way around. Sahara feels it—something that glows and makes her happy. She wants to say to the girl: I know who you are. I knew all along – you were *somebody's* daughter.... Instead, she asks, "Do you like Yeats?"

The girl laughs a self-conscious laugh. "I don't know what they are."

And Sahara smiles back in the dark. "Close your eyes and listen. It'll help you go to sleep."

She chants the words softly out into the night between them, one poem and then another, until the child beside her has fallen asleep. She goes on to finish, anyway,

"I will arise and go now, for always night and day
I hear lake water lapping with low sounds by the shore;
Where I stand on the roadway, or on the pavements grey,
I hear it in the deep heart's core."

Excerpts From Sunnyview Journal

Ann Viola

There is a cemetery that I used to pass often. Beside the grave of a child someone left toys. There were tricycles, dolls, even a miniature railroad village once. Each time I drove by I looked for the latest tribute, wishing I knew the person who lost that child. I would tell her that her example of love had deeply touched me. I also wondered what would be left at my grave under such circumstances, and I couldn't think of a thing. Now I can. First, there would be a gray van with the right front corner crushed in. Next someone could leave a hospital bed, complete with traction devices, or a surgical table. Later, a wheelchair would be appropriate, followed by a leg brace. Finally, this journal could be left there to tell the whole story to any curious onlooker.

When patients get together and talk it is like any other group of people. We keep the conversation light, skirting subjects that are too intense. Casual questions about our lives and families are the rule, as are complaints about the food or ordinary hassles. All the while we are watching one another carefully for signs of trouble or discouragement. If even one of my new friends gives up, then maybe I will. Their failures and their successes touch me, because I'm afraid I'm not going to survive here. Today a woman in physical therapy screamed while they stretched her knee. Tomorrow that might be me.

I wish my roommates would leave me alone. They are in their eighties, twice my age, and yet I have the role of 'mother' in this room. They complain to me about each other. I am supposed to settle things when they argue, or find lost eyeglasses, or call the nurses when they are needed, and so forth. These women accuse each other of stealing things when they have just misplaced them. I think this must be what it is like in a nursing home. I have to laugh or I would be shouting at them. Then, of course, they are offended with me for laughing at them. I can't win. I have to keep reminding myself that they have their pains and worries, too.

So many different nurses come in and out. I can't get their names straight. They have the same problems with us. One annoys me by calling us "Honey" or "Sweetie." "Sweetie" doesn't cut it as grease. I give her grief when she starts. Carol, the night nurse, is nice. She will rub my feet or wash my hair when I ask. It feels so good I have to be careful not to ask all the time. The male nurse is okay, but I can't get used to him. I'll burst my bladder before asking him for the bedpan. One of the day aides told me that she had been in an auto accident and lost half of her face. Two years of plastic surgery worked miracles. I cannot tell she was ever disfigured.

My visitors are dwindling. Five months is a long time to keep coming. In the beginning visitors were a strain on me. I had to pretend to be fine, keep up a cheerful attitude, or they would have been uncomfortable. Now they stay at home when I really need them. Of course I don't need the type who used to say they would never complain about their aches and pains after seeing me. A few of my friends are great, though, like Marion. She has been so faithful, and I hardly knew her before this happened. And Ginny, who is receiving chemotherapy treatments for breast cancer and never mentions her own anxiety in order to spare me. Some people I only vaguely knew from our church have come to see me, too. I wonder if I am their special service project, or if they visit because they really enjoy it.

Today was our 20th wedding anniversary. Hell of a place to celebrate. The nurses told me there would be a surprise for Ron and me this evening. It was wonderful. We were served a lovely steak dinner out on the sundeck with all of the trimmings. Then Ron was allowed to spend the night with me in a guest room on the third floor. My doctor also told me I can go home next weekend for a visit!

Physical therapy is miserable, yet that is why I am here. Three times a day I grit my teeth and bear the pain. When my therapist tells me I can do it, I never believe I can. Each task seems impossible at first. I look around me and see other patients struggling and decide to try harder. It's funny how it usually takes me three attempts before I do a particular action successfully. The first try is a disaster, the second an improvement, and by the third try I am actually able to do it. I just wish I would stop panicking at each new task. My therapist has so much patience with me. We work on pulling my right leg back, to stretch out my hip. I feel good with each bit of strength I gain, but I have far to go yet.

There are several young kids here. The nurses tell me many are victims of motorcycle or diving accidents. I see them by the elevators in the evenings. That is where they hang out, smoking and fooling around. They decorate their wheelchairs with junk I can't identify and listen to screaming music. They laugh a lot. It is a healthy sign, I think. The kid I worry about is the one who has to stay in bed. They have his head in a cage-like contraption screwed to his forehead. It must be torture. He is tall, about 15, and totally helpless. I never hear him talk, even to the nurses.

I had my visit home this weekend and expected to be happy. All it accomplished was more despair. How will I ever take care of my family again? I am going to be a burden to them. Danielle asked me if I was always going to be a "cripple," then she cried. I couldn't give her a comforting answer. I really don't know. And Lynne thinks I am dogging it, that I should be able to get right up and do things, be the same old mom. She is so angry with me she will not stay in the same room with me for more than five minutes. She doesn't seem to realize our lives are permanently changed. She thinks I've ruined her teenage years on purpose. She needs to see some of those spunky wheelchair kids. Then she might appreciate what she has. I'm angry, too.

Ron is very good to me. He set out some flowers for the porch planters and set me up to garden from the wheelchair. I covered myself with a towel, but was up to my elbows in dirt anyway. It was the nicest part of the weekend. Getting gritty was fun. Then Ron figured out a way for me to wash dishes. I teased him that it wasn't really my needs he had in mind. We have two plastic wash basins. He filled one with soapy water and the other with clear, for rinsing. He put the basins on the kitchen table and I went to work. I'm not so sure the dishes were clean enough, since my arm was tired from the planting, but my fingernails looked great!

I met a stroke patient today. His name is George and he said this was his third stroke. After each one his wife left him. She didn't want to take care of him. George is so bitter and needs attention. Somehow I feel I have to make up for his losses. There are so many tragic stories in this place. When someone finds a willing listener they pour out all the grief. I can't stand the injustice. As if living here for several weeks isn't enough, facing months of grueling therapy, dealing with the impact of a disabling condition, some have the added burden of rejection from the people they need the most. We all work darned hard for just a little progress. Where is our reward? Life smacks some of us in the face more than others. It is not fair. If there is anything I do not want to become after all of this, it is a "whiner." I want to be happy for the little things. I still have a life, even if it will be different. My mind is intact even if my body is a wreck. The people I really feel sorry for are the head-impaired. They have to learn so much over again. There is a young man here who is 25 and still believes himself to be 18, the age he was when he was injured.

I blew it today. My therapist was pressing me to do more and I couldn't stand it another minute. She lectured me, telling me how there are 100 people on a waiting list willing to work if I won't. Something inside of me let go. It was such a tiny feeling, like a button popping. But that button held in a whole garment, and once free everything let loose and I became completely unravelled. I yelled and thrashed around, hurting myself in the process. Bolts of pain seared my legs and I didn't care. I told everyone within the sound of my voice that I was nothing but a piece of human junk, so they might as well throw me away. I made a real spectacle of myself, and was ashamed later. I had insulted virtually every patient here. If I was junk, what were they? Carol, my night nurse, said I had experienced an "emotional catharsis." Nine months of pain, terror and anxiety were released in that explosion. I was limp and exhausted afterwards.

Dreams can be weird. Last night I dreamed I had no arms, but my legs were whole. A little boy came along and sliced his hand into my pocket, tugging for me to follow his lead. We went through some tangled, thorny bushes into a clearing. Ahead of us was a cottage that had been broken and smashed, as if by a terrible storm. I wanted to fix it, restore it to normal, but the amount of work was overwhelming. When I woke up I felt so depressed, as if the cottage was me and there was no one else to put it back together again.

Brendan, my attorney, came in to see me today. He was here to arrange to have my next therapy session videotaped for possible use in court. It was good to see him. But all he could talk about was his new baby. He is a nice man; very warm and friendly. I can't help wondering how much of his caring is real and how much is part of his professional demeanor. I'm really terrible. I find myself doubting the motives of anyone who comes to see me. My sense of self worth has taken a beating. Does a crippled person have anything to offer friends anymore? Will I just be a duty to people from now on? And what about Ron? Is he going to enjoy being married to a woman who will be a non-contributing partner? When we go places people will stare and feel sorry for him. How long will he be able to take it?

There is one amazing thing about this place. We are all united in an indelible way. It doesn't matter if you are old or young, black or white, well-educated or poor. We all root for one another, note every little bit of progress, drop the usual facades. There is Juckett, the man who weeps. I think nothing of holding his hand to give comfort to him. No one gossips about us. And Lottie, who has been told she must go to a nursing home rather than live with her daughter, as she had hoped. I admire Lottie. She never lets on to her daughter how disappointed she is. And Monna who laughs and cheers us all. There is such a flow of courtesy among these people. We all know each other on a level seldom possible in the outside world. I wish I could say as much for the staff. One of the thorns in my side is how patients are characterized by their disability. We are referred to as *quads*, *neuros*, *paras*, and *orthos*. Why not think of us as people? More than anything I just want to be normal. If I can't be normal, then I wish they would treat me as if I am. A wheelchair, a leg brace, crutches. Among all this equipment exists a person. Why can't they see the person? The other patients must feel the same way.

Something wonderful happened today. A patient down the hall named Tom walked for the first time in eight months. We all lined the corridor and cheered him on as he passed. Tom was radiant, full of the glory of the moment. I choked up, too. Tom will never know how grateful I am for him. If he can persist and win the battle, so can I. I see so much courage here that I can't allow my own circumstances to defeat me. I don't want to lose sight of that. Dealing with disability in the hospital is one thing. Dealing with it on the outside will be much tougher.

Ever since my "emotional catharsis" I've been seeing a staff psychologist. I've talked about all my fears and anger, my unresolved conflicts. He has helped me to put my life into perspective, to identify my priorities. For one thing, I need to be self-centered for a while, to serve my needs. I really haven't the energy to give my depleted emotional reserves the stress of anyone else's problems. For another, I have to accept that I cannot manipulate people or events, that I cannot shape the future. Precious little is in my hands. The future looms as unpredictably as the truck loomed that moment before I smashed into it. It is important for me to be prepared for the inevitable setbacks. I know I will be easily discouraged. I have to remember: third try and I can succeed, so I must never stop trying. The problem I need to address is, what will be my new identity? I want to contribute, to be effective. Will a disabled person be taken seriously? Will my friends be comfortable or pitying around me?

We're having a conference today. My doctor, nurse, therapists and family will gather to outline a plan for me for after my release. I have so many questions that no one can answer. I feel like a prisoner about to be let out of prison with no clothes, no money, no job, no resources. Freedom is intoxicating, but the reality is that a life has to be remade and enormous challenges overcome. Like the prisoner, my medical record will always follow me, my doctors will be my probation officers, and I will have to deal with prejudice and barriers. Leaving Sunnyview Hospital gives me an empty feeling I can't shake. A "what now" kind of vacuum. I wish I knew what will fill it.

We Are Ready

Marilyn Krysl

In the dream a man has built a house. He invites me inside, shows me white walls rising two stories, rooms opening into other rooms. When we reach the main room, a huge hall with vaulted ceiling, the man turns to me. The house is finished except for the floors, which are earth. My job, he tells me, is to plant the earth floors with grass. I kneel down and see at once that this ground isn't fertile topsoil. It's fine, powdered dirt, a mixture of crushed rock from deep in the earth's core and soil leached of all nutrients. Dead, barren earth.

Nothing has ever grown in it; nothing ever will. The job I'm responsible for is impossible. He has set me an impossible task.

In the dream the five of us are in a restaurant, crowded into a booth. I am between H, my husband, and our little girl, Ann. H plants one foot in the aisle to support himself and keep himself from slipping off the edge of the seat. On the other side our teenaged daughters, both of them big-boned and heavy, their shorts too tight, their blouses too small for their growing breasts. They fidget and twist, their hair swirling out as they flip their heads this way, then that. The booth barely holds them. They bump each other, both testy, then furious, each insisting the other is in the way.

As we eat we jab each other with our elbows. Now Ann accidentally spills a glass of milk. I am suddenly angry. They want us to come here, but they haven't provided adequate space. I am convinced the owner has purposely constructed the booths slightly below standard dimensions so that he can crowd more customers into his café, increase his profits. My children struggle to behave in a civilized way in this completely inadequate space. But I become more and more anxious. H is still eating, and I don't want to disturb him, but how, I wonder, will we manage?

I begin to sweat. Panic rises in my diaphragm and my throat constricts. The air is close, stale, and I cannot get enough into my lungs. Now a rat slinks across the aisle and disappears under the booth opposite me. *Excuse me,* I say to H, *Let me out please.* The pitch of my voice rises as I push against the table. Then I begin to push against H, gritting my teeth, repeating *you must let me out, I have to get out.*

In the dream the children are walking me to the bus stop. I don't know where I'm going but this is the last bus and I have to get on it. As we walk a hot wind begins to blow. It's a dry wind, a wind with fire in it. The buildings we pass are blasted, in ruins. It is a landscape of chunks of broken concrete, sidewalks buckled, steel bent, twisted, snapped, the blunt ends against a white sky.

I hold Ann's hand to keep her from stumbling, and with the other she lifts her skirt so that she won't trip. She looks up and smiles. She is pleased to be with me, close to me, and she's doing her best not to mind the wind and to hurry.

I remember how it was before, but I don't tell the children. I hope that if they don't know things were once different, if they believe the world was always like this, they won't be sad. I pretend these ruins are ordinary, that the wind is not brutal. I try to smile as the wind blows sand and grit against my skin, into my eyes.

Three Japanese, two men and a woman with a baby, board the bus. They are thin, nearly weightless, like pieces of silk the wind billows. They would burn instantly, I think to myself, and the wind spin their ashes across the sand.

I kiss each of the girls and step up behind the Japanese. Once on the bus I turn and look back. I am struck by how beautiful my children are, how small and perfectly formed. Now the woman's baby begins to cry, a sad wail, the cry of an old woman, heavy and broken by experience. How can this baby know so much, I wonder. How can I keep the truth from my children, for surely if they hear this baby crying, they will know I have been lying to them. I thought it was better for them if I lied to them, less painful. But now I regret this. By lying I have failed to prepare them for the life they must lead.

I decide I must get off the bus and tell them the truth

before I leave. But the door snaps shut and the bus begins to move. The girls wave as I press my hands and face against the window. Ann's mouth begins to curve into a smile—and then the blast. A flash of white light illuminates everything for the last time. It shines through flesh. I see, like three pressed flowers, the outlines of their bones.

In the force of the blast Ann's hair stands out from her skull.

In the dream I come home and find H has uprooted everything in the garden. Peas, beans, spinach, lettuce, carrots, all heaped in a pile, wilting beside the bare plot. I am incredulous. *Why* I ask H, wondering what special circumstances have forced him to do this. He is puzzled at my anger and answers matter-of-factly that he thought it was best. To him it's a minor matter. He was cleaning up, and it was time.

But it wasn't time, I'm certain of this. I continue to be unable to believe he's telling me the truth. My feelings swing recklessly from fury to grief and back to fury. I scream at him in rage. Then I begin to cry.

H is calm. He is still certain he has done the right thing. He frowns, puzzled, concerned at the excessiveness of my emotions. He understands that I'm upset, but he isn't really convinced my anger is justified.

Calmly he tries to console me, hoping I will soon be rational again.

In the dream the woman and I stand on a high ridge overlooking a valley. She is Chairwoman of the Department of History at the state university in the city where I live and she is a member of the City Council. She is blond, pretty, capable, professional, dressed for work in a trim, tailored suit, a leather purse slung over one shoulder.

She is neither my friend nor my enemy. I don't know her, except by reputation. All I have heard of her is favorable—she is intelligent, energetic, cheerful, generous, admired. But I am filled with fury at the fact of her existence. I am standing behind her, so close I can see the top of the zipper at the back of her blouse. I lunge, half turning her, getting my hands on her throat, choking her.

I am infused with astounding strength. The purse slips from her shoulder. In a few moments I've strangled her. Her body slumps onto the rocks at my feet. I look down at her body proud of my strength.

I am pleased with this murder.

I feel no remorse.

In the dream I am alone. But I am not just alone: I am the only one alive in the world at this time. I am making a row of rocks in the middle of a dirt road. I am doing this to mark the way for someone who will come later. I have to make sure that the rocks are close enough together to indicate a trail so that those who come later will be able to follow my progress and find me.

Carefully I place the rocks equal distances apart so that the trail will be easy to follow. Then it occurs to me that this regularity is monotonous. I decide to make an irregular pattern that will be interesting for those who will find it. I begin to place the rocks unequal distances apart, choosing each distance at random, without conscious repetition. As I work I become excited. The pattern is complicated, now quickening its rhythm, now stretching out in long, sweeping, repeating intervals. Those who follow me will quicken their pace, eagerly, appreciating the subtle nuances of my design.

I continue, knowing instinctively just what to do, certain that the pattern is beautiful and that it accurately portrays my own progress. I am completely happy. Before this I have not been happy, but now I know what happiness is.

In the dream the man stands before me, facing me, looking at me, waiting. He is neither patient nor impatient, and I feel no pressure from him to make one decision rather than another. He knows that he must delay his actions until I decide. So he looks at me and waits. I am conscious of time passing, but the more it passes the more there is. The light around us is golden, fertile light. It surrounds us and buoys us up. The light is almost tangible, and I imagine that I could pull away a handful.

There is a plenitude of thick, golden light, and I have infinite time in which to decide.

In the dream I am walking with another woman down the streets of the town where I grew up. The streets remain, but all of the houses and stores are gone. Around us is lush, rolling, open countryside.

I am not sad that the houses are gone; rather it seems that the earth is once again as it should be. Now it occurs to me that I want to make love to the woman who is with me, but I am afraid someone will see us. I look for a shelter, a clump of trees or a field of tall grass.

As I am looking we come upon my old grade school. Workmen are remodeling it, leaving some of the old parts intact, tearing down other parts, adding new wings, towers, windows, hallways. As I examine the work I also notice parts which are not new, but which I do not remember, which must have been added in my absence.

All that is happening here seems immensely important

to me. I am fascinated by what has changed and what has endured and by how old and new combine in one edifice. I wander through the building with my friend, pointing out to her each change, examining everything, noting each detail with wonder and pleasure.

Now a group of people approach us and invite us to join them on a bicycle ride through the countryside. We set out single file, heading west. As we meet two cars, the car in the rear tries to pass, nearly hits me, forces me into the ditch.

I am furious and I begin to scream angrily at the woman who tried to pass, berating her for nearly killing me. She looks at me and says, *but I can't see women riding bicycles.*

I am still more furious at this remark and I lecture her angrily, telling her she must see to her eyes because her blindness had nearly caused my death.

In the dream I walk along a ditch, desolate, nearly dry. A trickle of water in the muddy bottom. I pass the bodies of dead animals—a beaver on its back, bloated. Weasels, otters, all swollen to fantastic sizes, and now a great silver salmon, distended, belly up in the mud.

As I continue the ditch becomes a road.

At the edge of the road a snake, the first live animal. As I watch, the snake grows, and at the same time it raises itself, coil by abundant coil, into the air. Its scales shimmer as it lifts and turns, its enormous strength rolls slowly, surely through its length.

Beside the snake a girl, sitting on the ground. I recognize her as the one I've been looking for. *Look*, she says, pointing behind me, *the animals*. I turn and see them, some standing, others lying down, giraffes, elephants, lions and leopards, bear, antelope, horses, deer. Some of the mares have colts, and the lioness a litter of cubs. These animals have always shared the same grazing land, the same water. They have never known any other way of life. They are perfectly at peace with each other.

Now the leader, a bull elephant, begins to move. The animals lying down get up, the mares nudge their colts. I call to the girl and we go to meet them. They are enormous and wild, their bodies quivering, uncontrollable. They move slowly down the road, browsing grass at the road's edge, leaves and berries from the trees.

As they move we wander among them. We slide our backs against their hides, rub against their rough scales. We run our fingers through their fur. They nuzzle us gently with their soft lips. They lean into us. We lean into them. We make their sounds, we embrace their enormous flanks.

We move and move among them.

In the dream we sit on rock outcroppings, looking down at the ocean. The boy's hair is black, thick, curly. I am older than he is, but age doesn't matter anymore. There are only people, people of all ages, moving up and down the coast, staying close to the ocean, traveling through the moist air. Our clothes are old, second hand T-shirts, wool sweaters, soft faded jeans. Only my moccasins are new, and I am pleased with the softness of the deerskin and the way they fit my small feet perfectly. All we own we carry in two backpacks and a dufflebag. And on the ground beside the bike, two helmets. We are packed and ready to travel.

A light seabreeze blows inland. I climb down the rocks to the sand. In a car on the beach teenagers are necking and laughing, listening to smoky jazz on the radio. I am at ease, watching the ocean heave, and what I want to do is go on—go on walking this edge, in this air, hearing this music, listening to these human voices.

I look up and he signals that it's time to move on. I begin to climb the rocks. As I climb I feel the exactness, the inevitable deliberateness of my movements, the precision and absolute clarity of my perception. I am the one climbing and I am these things—the fact of my weight, the strength of my legs, arms, torso, and my own piercing breath.

There is nothing I am afraid of. Events have stripped me to the bone. At the time it often seemed events were too terrible to bear. I bore them. It seemed precious belongings were stripped from me, and that each loss was a small death. But in fact I did not die. I am alive and purified. Each time I thought I had lost something I became lighter and stronger and the muscle tone of my body took on tautness. Now superfluous layers are gone. Now my essential form stands out, clearly revealed.

I have been perfected by disaster. Now I am beautiful, sinewed, strong. I move up and up the rocks like a gazelle, sure and with swift, calm grace. I know everything I need to know. My energy is constant, my body hard with experience.

I never sleep.

It is sunset.

We are ready to go.

Don't Explain

Jewelle L. Gomez

Boston 1959

Letty deposited the hot platters on the table, effortlessly. She slid one deep-fried chicken, a club-steak with boiled potatoes and a fried porgie platter down her thick arm as if removing beaded bracelets. Each plate landed with a solid clink on the shiny formica, in its appropriate place. The last barely settled before Letty turned back to the kitchen to get Bo John his lemonade and extra biscuits and then to put her feet up. Out of the corner of her eye she saw Tip come in the lounge. His huge shoulders, draped in sharkskin, barely cleared the narow door frame.

"Damn! He's early tonight!" she thought but kept going. Tip was known for his generosity, that's how he'd gotten his nick-name. He always sat at Letty's station because they were both from Virginia, although neither had been back in years. Letty had come up to Boston in 1946 and been waiting tables in the 411 Lounge since '52. She liked the people: the pimps were limited but flashy; the musicians who hung around were unpredictable in their pursuit of a good time and the "business" girls were generous and always willing to embroider a wild story. After Letty's mother died there'd been no reason to go back to Burkeville.

Letty took her newspaper from the locker behind the kitchen and filled a large glass with the tart grapejuice punch for which the cook, Mabel, was famous.

"I'm going on break, Mabel. Delia's takin' my station."

She sat in the back booth nearest the kitchen beneath the large blackboard which displayed the menu. When Delia came out of the bathroom Letty hissed to get her attention. The reddish-brown skin of Delia's face was shiny with a country freshness that always made Letty feel a little warm.

"What's up, Miss Letty?" Her voice was soft and saucy.

"Take my tables for twenty minutes. Tip just came in."

The girl's already bright smile widened, as she started to thank Letty.

"Go 'head, go 'head. He don't like to wait. You can thank me if he don't run you back and forth fifty times."

Delia hurried away as Letty sank into the coolness of the overstuffed booth and removed her shoes. After a few sips of her punch she rested her head on the back of the seat with her eyes closed. The sounds around her were as familiar as her own breathing: squeaking Red Cross shoes as Delia and Vinnie passed, the click of high heels around the bar, the clatter of dishes in the kitchen and ice clinking in glasses. The din of conversation rose, levelled and rose again over the juke box. Letty had not played her record in days but the words spun around in her head as if they were on the turntable:

"...right or wrong don't matter
when you're with me sweet
Hush now, don't explain
You're my joy and pain."

Letty sipped her cool drink; sweat ran down her spine soaking into the nylon uniform. July weather promised to give no breaks and the fans were working over-time like everybody else.

She saw Delia cross to Tip's table again. In spite of the dyed red hair, no matter how you looked at her Delia was still a country girl: long and self-conscious, shy and bold because she didn't know any better. She'd moved up from Anniston with her cousin a year before and landed the job at the 411 immediately. She worked hard and sometimes Letty and she shared a cab going uptown after work, when Delia's cousin didn't pick them up in her green Pontiac.

Letty caught Tip eyeing Delia as she strode on long, tight-muscled legs back to the kitchen. "That lounge lizard!" Letty thought to herself. Letty had trained Delia: how to balance plates, how to make tips and how to keep the customer's hands on the table. She was certain Delia would have no problem putting Tip in his place. In the year she'd been working Delia hadn't gone out with any of the bar flies, though plenty had asked. Letty figured that Delia and her cousin must run with a different crowd. They talked to each other sporadically in the kitchen or during their break but Letty never felt that wire across her chest like Delia was going to ask her something she couldn't answer.

She closed her eyes again for the few remaining minutes. The song was back in her head and Letty had to squeeze her lips together to keep from humming aloud. She pushed her thoughts onto something else. But when she did she always stumbled upon Maxine. Letty opened her eyes. When she'd quit working at Salmagundi's and come to the 411 she'd promised herself never to think about any woman like that again. She didn't know why missing Billie so much brought it all back to her. She'd not thought of that time or those feelings for a while.

She heard Abe shout a greeting at Duke behind the bar as he surveyed his domain. That was Letty's signal. No matter whether it was her break or not she knew white people didn't like to see their employees sitting down, especially with their shoes off. By the time Abe was settled on his stool near the door, Letty was up, her glass in hand and on her way through the kitchen's squeaky swinging door.

"You finished your break already?" Delia asked.

"Abe just come in."

"Uh oh, let me git this steak out there to that man. Boy he sure is nosey!"

"Who, Tip?"

"Yeah, he ask me where I live, who I live with, where I come from like he supposed to know me!"

"Well just don't take nothing he say to heart and you'll be fine. And don't take no rides from him!"

"Yeah, he asked if he could take me home after I get off. I told him me and you had something to do."

Letty was silent as she sliced the fresh bread and stacked it on plates for the next orders.

"My cousin's coming by, so it ain't a lie, really. She can ride us."

"Yeah," Letty said as Delia giggled and turned away with her platter.

Vinnie burst through the door like she always did, looking breathless and bossy. "Abe up there, girl! You better get back on station. You got a customer."

Letty drained her glass with deliberation, wiped her hands on her thickly starched white apron and walked casually past Vinnie as if she'd never spoken. She heard Mabel's soft chuckle float behind her. She went over to Tip who was digging into the steak like his life depended on devouring it before the plate got dirty.

"Everything alright tonight?" Letty asked, her ample brown body towering over the table.

"Yeah, baby, everything alright. You ain't workin' this side no more?"

"I was on break. My feet can't wait for your stomach, you know."

Tip laughed. "Break! What you need a break for, big and healthy as you is!"

"We all gets old, Tip. But the feet get old first, let me tell you that!"

"Not in my business, baby. Why you don't come on and work for me and you ain't got to worry 'bout your feet."

Letty sucked her teeth loudly, the exaggeration a part of the game they played over the years. "Man, I'm too old for that mess!"

"You ain't too old for me."

"Ain't nobody too old for you! Or too young neither, looks like."

"Where you and that gal goin' tonight?"

"To a funeral," Letty responded dryly.

"Aw woman get on away from my food!" The gold cap on his front tooth gleamed from behind his greasy lips when he laughed. Letty was pleased. Besides giving away money Tip liked to hurt people. It was better when he laughed.

The kitchen closed at 11:00 p.m. Delia and Letty slipped out of their uniforms in the tiny bathroom and were on their way out the door by 11:15. Delia looked even younger in her knife-pleated skirt and white cotton blouse. Letty did feel old tonight in her slacks and long-sleeved shirt. The movement of car headlights played across her face, which was set in exhaustion. The dark green car pulled up and they slipped in quietly, both anticipating tomorrow, Sunday, the last night of their work week.

Delia's cousin was a stocky woman who looked forty, Letty's age. She never spoke much. Not that she wasn't friendly. She always greeted Letty with a smile and laughed at Delia's stories about the customers. "Just close to the chest like me, that's all," Letty often thought. As they pulled up to the corner of Columbus Avenue and Cunard Street Letty opened the rear door. Delia turned to her and said, "I'm sorry you don't play your record on your break no more, Miss Letty. I know you don't want to, but I'm sorry just the same."

Delia's cousin looked back at them with a puzzled expression but said nothing. Letty slammed the car door shut and turned to climb the short flight of stairs to her apartment. Cunard Street was quiet outside her window and the guy upstairs wasn't blasting his record player for once. Still, Letty lie awake and restless in her single bed. The fan was pointed at the ceiling, bouncing warm air over her, rustling her sheer nightgown.

Inevitably the strains of Billie Holiday's songs brushed against her, much like the breeze that fanned around her. She felt silly when she thought about it, but the melodies gripped her like a solid presence. It was more than the music. Billie had been her hero. Letty saw Billie as big, like herself, with big hungers, and some secret that she couldn't tell anyone. Two weeks ago, when Letty heard that the Lady had died, sorrow enveloped her. A refuge had been closed that she could not consciously identify to herself or to anyone. It embarrassed her to think about. Like it did when she remembered Maxine.

When Letty first started working at the 411 she met Billie when she'd come into the club with several musicians on her way back from the Jazz Festival. There the audience, curious to see what a real, live junkie looked like, had sat back waiting for Billie to fall on her face. Instead she'd killed them dead with her liquid voice and rough urgency. Still, the young, thin horn player kept having to reassure her: "Billie you were the show, the whole show!"

Once convinced, Billie became the show again, loud and commanding. She demanded her food be served at the bar and sent Mabel, who insisted on waiting on her personally, back to the kitchen fifteen times. Billie laughed at jokes that Letty could barely hear as she bustled back and forth between the abandoned kitchen and her own tables. The sound of that laugh from the bar penetrated her bones. She'd watched and listened, certain she saw something no one else did. When Billie had finished eating and gathered her entourage to get back on the road she left a tip, not just for Mabel but for each of the waitresses and the bartender. "Generous just like the 'business' girls," Letty was happy to note. She still had the two one dollar bills in an envelope at the back of her lingerie drawer.

After that, Letty felt even closer to Billie. She played one of the few Lady Day records on the juke box every night, during her break. Everyone at the 411 had learned not to bother her when her song came on. Letty realized, as she lay waiting for sleep, that she'd always felt that if she had been able to say or do something that night to make friends with Billie, it might all have been different. In half sleep the faces of Billie, Maxine and Delia blended in her mind. Letty slid her hand along the soft nylon of her gown to rest it between her full thighs. She pressed firmly, as if holding desire inside herself. Letty could have loved her enough to make it better. That was Letty's final thought as she dropped off to sleep.

Sunday nights at the 411 were generally mellow. Even the pimps and prostitutes used it as a day of rest. Letty came in early and had a drink at the bar and talked with the bartender before going to the back to change into her uniform. She saw Delia through the window as she stepped out of the green Pontiac, looking as if she'd just come from Concord Baptist Church. "Satin Doll" was on the juke box, wrapping the bar in cool nostalgia.

Abe let Mabel close the kitchen early on Sunday and Letty looked forward to getting done by 10:00 or 10:30, and maybe enjoying some of the evening. When her break time came Letty started for the juke box automatically. She hadn't played anything by Billie in two weeks; now, looking down at the inviting glare, she knew she still couldn't do it. She punched the buttons that would bring up Jackie Wilson's "Lonely Teardrops" and went to the back booth.

She'd almost dropped off to sleep when she heard Delia whisper her name. She opened her eyes and looked up into the girl's smiling face. Her head was haloed in tight, shiny curls.

"Miss Letty, won't you come home with me tonight?"

"What?"

"I'm sorry to bother you, but your break time almost up. I wanted to ask if you'd come over to the house tonight ... after work. My cousin'll bring you back home after."

Letty didn't speak. Her puzzled look prompted Delia to start again.

"Sometime on Sunday my cousin's friends from work come over to play cards, listen to music, you know. Nothin' special, just some of the girls from the office building down on Winter Street where she work, cleaning. She, I mean we, thought you might want to come over tonight. Have a drink, play some cards...."

"I don't play cards much."

"Well not everybody play cards ... just talk ... sitting around talking. My cousin said you might like to for a change."

Letty wasn't sure she liked the last part: "for a change," as if they had to entertain an old aunt.

"I really want you to come, Letty. They always her friends but none of them is my own friends. They alright, I don't mean nothin' against them, but it would be fun to have my own personal friend there, you know?"

Delia was a good girl. Those were the perfect words to describe her, Letty thought smiling. "Sure honey, I'd just as soon spend my time with you as lose my money with some fools."

They got off at 10:15 and Delia apologized that they had to take a cab uptown. Her cousin and her friends didn't work on Sunday so they were already at home. Afraid that the snag would give Letty an opportunity to back out Delia hadn't mentioned it until they were out of their uniforms and on the sidewalk. Letty almost declined, tempted to go home to the safe silence of her room. But she didn't. She stepped into the street and waved down a

Red and White cab. All the way uptown Delia apologized that the evening wasn't a big deal and cautioned Letty not to expect much. "Just a few friends, hanging around, drinking and talking." She was jumpy and Letty tried to put her at ease. She had not expected her first visit would make Delia so anxious.

The apartment was located halfway up Blue Hill Avenue in an area where a few blacks had recently been permitted to rent. They entered a long, carpeted hallway and heard the sounds of laughter and music ringing from the rooms at the far end.

Once inside, with the door closed, Delia's personality took on another dimension. This was clearly her home and Letty could not believe she ever really needed an ally to back her up. Delia stepped out of her shoes at the door and walked to the back with her same, long-legged gait. They passed a closed door, which Letty assumed to be one of the bedrooms, then came to a kitchen ablaze with light. Food and bottles were strewn across the pink and gray formica-top table. A counter opened from the kitchen into the dining room, which was the center of activity. Around a large mahogany table sat five women in smoke-filled concentration, playing poker.

Delia's cousin looked up from her cards with the same slight smile as usual. Here it seemed welcoming, not guarded as it did in those brief moments in her car. She wore brown slacks and a matching sweater. The pink, starched points of her shirt collar peeked out at the neck.

Delia crossed to her and kissed her cheek lightly. Letty looked around the table to see if she recognized anyone. The women all seemed familiar in the way that city neighbors can, but Letty was sure she hadn't met any of them before. Delia introduced her to each one: Karen, a short, round woman with West Indian bangles up to her pudgy elbow; Betty, who stared intently at her cards through thick eyeglasses encased in blue cat-eye frames; Irene, a big, dark woman with long black hair and a gold tooth in front. Beside her sat Myrtle who was wearing army fatigues and a gold Masonic ring on her pinky finger. She said hello in the softest voice Letty had ever heard. Hovering over her was Clara, a large red woman whose hair was bound tightly in a bun at the nape of her neck. She spoke with a delectable southern accent that drawled her "How're you doin' " into a full paragraph that was draped around an inquisitive smile.

Delia became ill-at-ease again as she pulled Letty by the arm toward the French doors behind the players. There was a small den with a desk, some books and a television set. Through the next set of glass doors was a livingroom. At the record player was an extremely tall, brown-skinned woman. She bent over the wooden cabinet searching for the next selection, oblivious to the rest of the gathering. Two women sat on the divan in deep conversation, which they punctuated with constrained giggles.

"Maryalice, Sheila, Dolores ... this is Letty."

They looked up at her quickly, smiled, then went back to their pre-occupations: two to their gossip, the other returned to the record collection. Delia directed Letty back toward the foyer and the kitchen.

"Come on, let me get you a drink. You know, I don't even know what you drink!"

"Delia?" Her cousin's voice reached them over the counter, just as they stepped into the kitchen. "Bring a couple of beers back when you come, OK?"

"Sure, babe." Delia went to the refrigerator and pulled out two bottles. "Let me just take these in. I'll be right back."

"Go 'head, I can take care of myself in this department, girl." Letty surveyed the array of bottles on the table. Delia went to the dining room and Letty mixed a Scotch and soda. She poured slowly as the reality settled on her. These women were friends, perhaps lovers, like she and Maxine had been. The name she'd heard for women like these burst inside her head: bulldagger. Letty flinched, angry she had let it in, angry that it frightened her. "Ptuh!" Letty blew air through her teeth as if spitting the word back at the air.

She did know these women, Letty thought, as she stood at the counter smiling out at the poker game. They were oblivious to her, except for Terry. Letty remembered that was Delia's cousin's name. As Letty took her first sip, Terry called over to her. "We gonna be finished with this game in a minute Letty, then we can talk."

"Take your time," Letty said, then went out through the foyer door and around to the livingroom. She walked slowly on the carpet and adjusted her eyes to the light, which was a bit softer. The tall woman, Maryalice, had just put a record on the turntable and sat down on a love seat across from the other two women. Letty stood in the doorway a moment before the tune began:

"Hush now, don't explain
Just say you'll remain
I'm glad you're back
Don't explain..."

Letty was stunned, but the song sounded different here, among these women. Billie sang just to them, here. The isolation and sadness seemed less inevitable with these women listening. Letty watched Maryalice sitting with her long legs stretched out tensely in front of her. She was wrapped in her own thoughts, her eyes closed. She appeared curiously disconnected, after what had clearly been a long search for this record. Letty watched her face as she swallowed several times. Then Letty moved to sit on the seat beside her. They listened to the music while the other two women spoke in low voices.

When the song was over Maryalice didn't move. Letty rose from the sofa and went to the record player. Delia stood tentatively in the doorway of the livingroom. Letty picked up the arm of the phonograph and replaced it at the beginning of the record. When she sat again beside Maryalice she noticed the drops of moisture on the other woman's lashes. Maryalice relaxed as Letty settled onto the seat beside her. They both listened to Billie together, for the first time.

The Chipko

Sally Miller Gearhart

Garland was squatting over a shallow hole in the carpet of pine needles, contemplating the woes of the human species and trying to face her own possible impending death. Shitting was not only good civil disobedience protocol—in case they brought in sonarbowel units; it also called up in her the creatively philosophical, and particularly so now that dying seemed such a sudden and extreme reality. As usual, she had begun her morning contemplation with the immediate material circumstances: the dark pre-dawn sky, the cool woods, the nearby preparations for a violent confrontation, her own present—rather strained—position in the scheme of things. And as usual she had leapt immediately to broad overarching universal concepts (good-and-evil, motion-and-rest, being-and-nothingness) that forced her this time to take refuge in "Hamlet." She pushed her sphincter muscle hard trying to force out the dregs of yesterday's rice and sprouts, then tightened it again beginning the series of clean-up contractions. The Prince of Denmark accompanied her. "...Their cur. Rents turn. A wry. And lose. The name. Of ac. Tion." She uttered the last words aloud and, wiping herself with a sheaf of broadoak leaves, she rose triumphantly to pull up her pants and step to the side of the hole. There was just enough light to guide her proper covering of her accomplishment. She made her formulary bows: one of gratitude to the Receiving Mother and one of appreciation to her body for its miraculous processes.

She picked her way carefully back to the temporary camp that crowded the small meadow. Beyond it and over a rise lay the gentle hillside that they would be defending in a few hours. She could make out now the slow-moving forms of other early risers—or un-sleepers—pulling themselves erect, bulky shadows trying to tiptoe through still-filled sleeping bags. The group had grown, she noted, even during the night. The expanse of bedrolls covered the whole eastern end of the clearing and extended itself well into the trees.

As she watched the camp come to life she wondered how many times in this world's history it had been women who had awakened early on the day of a battle and stood in a quiet dawn to dread or hope or remember or wonder. For there were mostly women and children here for this chipko, just as there had been twenty-five years ago when the first whole forest had been saved by such a demonstration. Most of the weave-schemes called for the ultimate protection of anyone under twelve, but a surprising number of six- and seven-year olds had refused to be banished from the action; Garland wasn't convinced that either they or their mothers knew how nasty this confrontation was going to be.

"So are you any good with dogs?" Ellen was behind her, holding out to her a mug of something steaming.

"Okay. No better than the next person. Why?"

"They heard we were spiking trees. It's not true but they're royally pissed anyway. So they're bringing dogs today. Maluma just found out. Said to pass the word."

"I heard it was going to be whirley-birds." Garland sipped her tea and then set it aside to stretch her back and her legs. "Have they ever used air support here?"

"No. And I doubt that they will. The only thing they could drop that would wilt us and not the loggers is mace bags and even Champion International's not going to spring for gas masks for all those loggers." Ellen flung tea dregs onto one of the clumps of low-growing feeder grass and rested her cup on a stump. "I don't know what could stop helicopters. Unless maybe the flying furies could scare the bejesus out of them."

Garland looked up. She didn't know Ellen well enough to discern a joke in her manner. "You believe in them? Women who can fly?"

"I'd like to. Wouldn't you?"

"When we heard about this chipko we sent word about it to some women in Western Michigan. Never heard back from them. There are supposed to be flying furies down there."

"Well, if there are flying furies anywhere it would be in Western Michigan. I think it's one big fantasy, myself. I only talk about them to keep my spirits up."

"Yeah," Garland said. Then she drew her oakheart

fighting stick from its six-foot cotton sheath. "I'm not sure I'm ready for this," she mused. "The only chipkos I've done were mild compared to what they described last night. Nobody got hurt bad, much less killed."

"So the bluffs have been called and the peaceful parts are over. The jacks are more desperate. They're pushed to feed their kids. 'I'm just following orders, ma'am,' as he pulls his starter cord. They won't use the battery-driven chain saws, you know. Too quiet. Not enough snarl. The gentlemen we'll be seeing today get their contrachipko training from the N.R.A. Here, let me show you the routine."

She took up her own long inch-round stick, silently addressed it by name and then assumed an alert-rest fighting stance. She moved swiftly then into a series of quick sword-strikes with high blocks. Bending almost to a squat she established an internal pattern of low reverses and knee-breakers and then climaxed with a wide shoulder-high backhand sweep. She ended in the classic absorption stance with her stave extended at head level in the Embrace of the Enemy. The seducement of that energy drew even Garland off-balance and in toward Ellen's center.

Garland bowed and spoke silently to her stick, addressing it by name, and stroking its familiar smoothness. "Obeah, Fear-Striker, you are wood to protect wood today." She crossed a whole ocean and half a continent to remember the quiet island grove where the stick had its origin. What a contrast to today's wholesale cutting! There there had been public prayers, rituals, consultations (inter- and intra-species) before any tree could be cut. And when the moment came, what tears were there, what lamentations! Then finally what celebrations of the new trees planted in the shadow of the fallen! She stepped behind Ellen. "Once more, por favor."

They spent the dawn rehearsing the stickmatrix's moves, those precise coordinated attacks designed to rob woodcutters of their machines without seriously injuring the woodcutter. The stickmatrix was the only element of chipko strategy that could be called offensive. Characteristically it went into action only after a tree (or a person) had actually been touched by a faller or a saw. But its preliminary kata, done in unison at the first moment of real threat, was distinctly aggressive and often formidable enough—like the maw of a great whale, some suggested—to give even the largest saw a sputter. More than one crew of loggers had succumbed, before any blow was struck, to the vision of twelve women (the Goddess made thirteen, and the sticks made them seem like a legion) advancing toward them in a wave of mysterious open power. It was this kata that Garland practiced with Ellen until dawn became sunrise, and until some unnamed figure refilled their cups with a strong nightshade tea for the last time.

Close to a hundred women and children, with a few men, were exiting the meadow and slipping into the woods over the rise, a peace-obsessed army, moving almost noiselessly to the shelter of an oak grove. There they relieved the night watchers and the changing body of scouts who reported from both directions along the dirt road on low-rev motorcycles or on the bicycles that sacrificed speed for silence.

The Weavers, the main body of the company, took their assigned places on the perimeter of the cutting site, just across from the clearing on the other side of the road where a yellow crane, its boom towering upward, sat on a large flatbed. Another flatbed held a Number 8 Cat. On the ground, a smaller bulldozer waited patiently to do its task. It was there in the clearing that the trucks would draw up to discharge the logging crews. The Weavers, in groups of friends, lovers, or families, surrounded sets of trees, intertwining their anger, their passion, their love, their stubbornness. From that phalanx rose a protective shield that extended toward the as-yet empty road.

A group that had come to be called the Stillers mingled with the Weavers but differed in their task. They were to reach out mentally to the oncoming fallers, calming anger, damping wild and otherwise unpredicted actions that individual men often resorted to. Garland had once seen a logger, crazed by his thwarted attempts to cut the women's fighting sticks, actually turn his revved chain saw on one of his fellow loggers. Stillers had saved the near-victim's life in that instance—and perhaps that of the attacker. The Stillers certainly didn't give the impression that they were participating in the confrontations. Usually they hovered behind the Weavers looking very tranced-out. Most chipkos, however, and for that matter most operative non-violent groups, refused these days to do an action without some Stillers, so much had they come to depend upon them.

Both Stiller and Weaver maintained maximum flexibility in their positions so that they could accommodate any shifts in the direction of the attack. And both Stiller and Weaver were ultimately committed to the oldest strategy of all, if it came to that: hugging individual trees, there to stay until that tree's life was no longer threatened.

Moving back and forth among them all was Maluma, a strange kind of military genius, clad quite practically in boots and soft cotton from toe to chin and wearing from her chin up a wild headdress of brightly colored bird-feathers. "Though maybe that's battle dress, too," Garland reminded herself. Maluma quizzed her lieutenants on plans and counterplans, carried babies from one parent to another, hugged or joked with her troops as occasion allowed, and recited with one or another of them: "I protect these trees. I protect myself. I protect my comrades. I protect him who attacks us. I will not be moved." Over the decades those words had become chipko Weavers' haunting chant.

Garland had forgotten that she was going to die today. Instead she was fascinated all over again by the steadiness, the assurance, of these weaponless warriors and their leader. Her own adrenalin was already lifting her high, making her feet move up and down in soft stomps of anticipation. Deliberately she closed her eyes. "Broad. Low. Easy. Slow," she told herself. Obeah pulsed with her as she retarded her rhythm.

An old Yamaha geared down over its driver's shouts that eleven pickups and jeeps plus panel trucks and a string of larger rigs were less than nine minutes away to the west, an estimated thirty loggers. And more could be expected from the east. There was a stir among the waiting Weavers and Stillers, a lift to the beginning day, and a murmur in the tops of the oak trees. As she stepped through roadside briars Garland found herself scanning the early morning blue above the clearing. Her mind conjured a skyful of pairs of Amazons flying side-by-side, a war-cry on their lips, descending upon the forest. "Hope springs eternal," she muttered grimly.

Clarion was collecting fighting sticks for the blessing, her actions now shot through with a sense of immediacy. Thirteen women were gathered around her, more than those needed for the katas, but not enough to form a semi-matrix. The three extras would probably stand with the Weavers as replacements for the matrix when it was moving as a unit. They would join actively when the matrix broke for any individual fighting.

Garland failed to calm her racing heart as she entered the ring of women next to Ellen, adding her own stick to the ones that Clarion was holding on end in the center of the circle: fifteen wooden staves of varying lengths, hues, textures, and degrees of use, each with stories to tell, each marked in some indelible way with the identity of the woman whose spirit extended through it. Garland looked around the circle, trying to match staves with women.

She joined her hands to the battle sashes of the women beside her and her voice to the rising incantation. They called up the rage of the earth, the suffering of every beaten woman, the death of every witch and that of her familiar, the agony of burning faggots, the strength of the roots, trunks, limbs, buds, leaves, and fruit of every tree from alpha to omega. They upturned the gathered rods and set them vertical again, then addressed their destined paths according to the four directions, eight planes, and seven modes of swiftness. They sang for the moment of Quickening in the conflict, the moment at which they would know that the birthing of victory, however pained, would be sure and sweet. They thanked the wands for their protective power, prayed that any injury they brought would heal around a seed of change, and reclaimed their weapons with a shout that Weavers and Stillers joined.

The sound of the first motor came just behind the last three scouts, two of them cyclists. "The dogs are in the panel trucks," one reported, drawing her bike behind the line of Weavers. A wave of consternation passed over the gathering. One woman and two small crying girls withdrew to the top of the hill. The women in the stick matrix assumed a first form position standing with their staves at rest.

Trucks of all sizes began pulling into the clearing or parking on the roadside. The sheriff tumbled out of one pick-up, a journalist with a tape recorder from another. Enthusiasm was pouring out of the cabs like the home team from the locker room at playoffs. A man in a grey workshirt with rolled-up sleeves lurched out of the lead truck. He took off his Big Tar cap and shifted his clipboard to wipe his brow.

"Who's in charge?" he called out, stepping toward the trees he wanted to cut. When only silence greeted him he motioned to one of the other drivers. "Roy!" Then to the lines of humans standing between him and his livelihood he said, "I want to talk with your head woman. And don't give me any of that equal stuff. Somebody's got to be responsible."

Maluma pulled away from the Weavers and advanced toward him. Growling trucks and slamming cab doors drowned out what they said to each other. Garland saw the big man gesturing toward Roy, and Roy speaking to Maluma. Maluma shook her head. One of the men kicked a chain saw on. A burst of raucous laughter charged the air. "Guys, cut it!" shouted Grey Shirt. The chain saw died. Maluma turned and walked back to the lines of Weavers.

Grey Shirt raised his voice in the growing silence. "This is your last chance, all of you. We have to get to these trees and we have a court order that backs us. I'm asking you once to leave quietly. Go back home and have some breakfast." Pause. "I'm asking you twice: please leave so we can cut the timber." Pause. "This is the third time: you have to leave peaceably so we can do our job."

No one moved, including Grey Shirt. Then he jerked his head toward the men behind him and sliced the air with his clipboard. The loggers broke into action. Doors to the panel trucks were flung open and pairs of large fighting dogs began straining on leashes in front of strong men. Chain saw motors tore into the silence. With remarkable timing, more trucks heaved into view from the east side of the hill. They too spilled out waves of shouting men with saws at ready, motors revving, chains flashing in their endless circling. Now from both edges of the cutting site dogs were goaded into snarls and rough barks. They converged on the human barrier confronting them and filled the morning with fury.

Garland felt rather than saw the wave of activity surging toward her. Then she was lost in the swirl of the matrix as it began its move, internally at first, and then with concentrated overt focus. A contingent of women with spinning wands danced in unison onto the road, intoning a barely audible hum. Startled woodsmen and their dogs hesitated and then drove forward again toward the matrix only to halt when the women broke into a concave double semi-circle of raised sticks: the Embrace of the Enemy. For a second the chaos of barks and motors ceased. The forest and all its occupants stood in tiptoe anticipation. Then in the throat of the matrix the hum grew to full voice, a ki-ay growing louder, and louder still, threatening at last to split the silence. Just short of its climax, one of the fallers shouted, "Don't fall for it, men! It's a trick! Move! Move! They can't sustain it! Move, I tell you!"

The spell broke, and with its shattering a new roar of cacaphony descended. Garland was dimly aware that the chaos sounded different but before she could decide the reason a sixteen-inch chain saw whipped up and toward her. She sidestepped, driving Obeah's far end into a soft solar plexus. Her attacker doubled over at an angle precisely designed to let her slip her stick into the brake guard and lever the machine out of his hands. To her left Ellen delivered a knee-breaker to the advance of another logger, this one reaching with outstretched blade to a forward standing juvenile oak. All around her a set-to raged. Men shouted, saws roared, Weavers chanted, dogs—no, there were no dogs barking! That was the difference! Dogs, in fact, had simply stopped moving. They sat or lay in the road in an almost reverent silence, regarding the women. No amount of hauling or kicking could stir them. Dobermans, Shepherds and Pit Bulls, expensively and ruthlessly trained to be ferocious, were refusing to attack. Garland noted a single exception: one Shepherd was actually wagging its tail and attempting to drag its leasher toward the loud-chanting Weavers.

Fallers who were not angrily and futilely urging stolid animals into action were shouting twice as loud, squaring their shoulders twice as stiffly, and advancing with redoubled determination toward the scattered matrix and beyond it toward the oaks. In a shift of strategy, two of them would force a Weaver from a tree, holding her helpless or at times immobilizing her with ropes while a third attempted a jump cut on the rough old trunk. He would be foiled by another body that immediately wrapped itself around the tree. And again: pull her away, rev the idle, step to cut, and find another body inches from the blade. And again and again throughout the forest.

Garland, with other stick-fighters attempting to stave off the onslaught of men with saws, looked when she could toward the Weavers and their attackers. In an instant before he attempted again to cut, she saw one faller trying by force of long experience to keep his blade from nearing human flesh. His face rang a host of changes—contempt, braggadocio, conflict, fear, anguish, frustration, and finally rage and dogged determination. He brought the spinning chain a centimeter from a bare shoulder and then jerked it high above his head as he shrieked, "Get her AWAAAAAAAY!"

A constant flow of chanting Weavers was appearing from nowhere to replace those dragged back from the trees. Those dragged back, once released, flung themselves around yet other trees. Garland found herself praying that the good luck would hold, that they would continue to see no blood, that the fallers would give up ... that the figure stalking toward her with raised and revved saw would go for her outflung stick and not for her belly button.

The man in fact went for the stick, a wild concentration propelling him onward, an ugly smile marring his face. Garland pushed her breath into Obeah, focusing entirely upon the slow drawing of her attacker around, around, and yet further around until she saw his intent to charge. At that moment she swung the stick behind her, twirling tightly and executing the perfect veronica. The logger lunged and stumbled. Then with a frantic scream he toppled to the ground, twisting so that he saved his chest but not his forearm from the still fully-throttled spinning chain. Garland got the blood full in her face, and shocked herself by licking and savoring its saltiness before she dropped upon the ignition switch to kill the motor.

The man was shrieking, and jerking in uncontrolled spasms that flung his truncated limb repeatedly against her breast. She determined to ignore what lay before her eyes:

a shirtsleeve that couched a severed wrist. Instead she grabbed the flailing stump and secured it against her. Then with her full torso she covered him and blocked out the noise and chaos that pounded around them. Gently she held the unresisting body below her and pushed slow extensions into it. The body eased. Garland eased. She looked up then to call for help only to discover above her the forms of two large men. Without conscious thought she reached for her stick. She stopped her motion as one man shook his head. "We'll take him," he said.

"You need to stop the blood," she said, shifting to her feet.

He nodded. "We'll take him," he said again.

In the rising mid-morning light, in the interstices of a two-stroke heartbeat and over the inert body of one fallen in the fray, three people searched each other's faces for signs of understanding. Then one of them, partly to hide the rising of very inappropriate tears, turned her back and plunged toward the jungle of sound where lines were clearly drawn and friends and enemies were more easily identified.

Garland had just joined an embattled Clarion and two other stick fighters in their defense of a tree called Big Mama Oak when she realized that there had been a distinct change in the whole encounter. Her heart sank when she saw that the battle had shifted, and why. The men, almost as many now as those who opposed them, had begun imprisoning the non-resistant women in huge army trucks so that very slowly the number of those who returned to protect the trees was dwindling. Garland could see a cordon of guards surrounding the trucks. They beat down with ax handles and threatened with aggressive chain saws the heads and arms that poked through the high cloth covering of the truckbeds. "Come on!" Garland shouted, pulling Clarion toward that scene.

They clashed head-on with two men trying to force Maluma into a truck. Garland rejoiced to see that Weaver and Stiller tactics had changed now from pure passive non-resistance to an active effort to get back to the trees. She rejoiced a second time when Maluma released a wild cry that stunned her keepers and gave Clarion a chance to thrust her stick across one man's Adam's apple, thus pinning him against the side of the truck. At the same moment Garland brought Obeah down on the knuckles of the other faller and twisted the lower end of the stick upward to wedge beneath his jawbone. From there she levered him off the ground and into a feet-over-head spin that landed him unconscious several yards away.

Clarion and Maluma were trying to get near the long bolt that imprisoned the people in the truck and Garland was about to throw an attacker who had conveniently grabbed her stick. But all of them froze like statues at the sound of a collective shout of joy. It ascended from a wedge of loggers slowly approaching Big Mama Oak. Already the twenty or so remaining Weavers and Stillers were being seized and tied by groups of men. However hard they struggled in their new-found active resistance they could not break free or reach their beloved trees. Toward the center of the grove the remaining members of the matrix fought a losing battle against a sheer mass of men who moved calmly over them, disarming them, securing them to trees with their own battle sashes.

Intoxicated by such promise of success the men in the wedge were laughing now, pushing forward behind a confident logger who led the way toward the old oak. "Take the big old one first, Pierre! Let 'em see her fall!" "Watch, ladies, watch. She'll make such fine panelling for your house!"

As Garland leapt forward, large men closed in on her, surrounding her and her companions. As she lost her stick she managed to duck her chin and avoid a neck lock. She relaxed into a low energy-gathering stance and with all of Mother Earth beneath and within her she raised her hands in front of her face, dragging with them the protesting arms of the man who held her from behind. She knelt, and with a surge of power swept her assailant over her head and into the path of another oncoming man, thus leaving her own arms free to receive and dispatch her third attacker. But there was a fourth. And a fifth. And a tenth.

She broke beneath their weight and sank to the ground. With what she knew would be her last free breath she hurled a curse at the cordon of men approaching the unprotected tree. As the mass of logger flesh descended on her breathless body she discovered a chink that gave her a view of the ultimate defeat.

She saw Pierre raise his chain saw. His company of men cheered. He placed its blade close by the bark of the old oak—knee-high, so the Cat could later have a purchase on the stump. The men cheered again. He revved the motor and began the slanting bite into the wood.

A rock the size of a fist struck the chain saw from Pierre's hands and drove it into the dirt. The cordon of loggers was peppered with a rain of human bodies. The men fell back, overwhelmed by a sudden foe.

From out of nowhere a war-cry split the air. And Garland felt her burdens lift. As man after man was pulled from atop her, as breath after blessed breath went coursing through her hungry lungs, she craned her neck upward toward the midmorning sun.

The sky was full of women.

Contributors' Notes

Margaret Atwood is well known as an editor, poet, essayist, short story writer and novelist. Her novels include *The Edible Woman*, *Surfacing*, *Lady Oracle*, *Life Before Man*, *Bodily Harm* and *The Handmaid's Tale*, which received numerous awards when it was published in 1986.

Toni Cade Bambara edited *The Black Woman: An Anthology*, in 1974. Since then, her short stories have appeared in many journals and anthologies. She has published two volumes of short stories, *Gorilla, My Love* and *The Sea Birds Are Still Alive*, as well as a novel, *The Salt Eaters* (all with Random House).

Becky Birtha is a black lesbian feminist fiction writer and poet. Her stories have appeared in several feminist anthologies and in two of her own collections: *For Nights Like This One: Stories of Loving Women* (Frog In The Well) and *Lovers' Choice* (The Seal Press).

Sally Miller Gearhart is the author of *The Wanderground: Stories of the Hill Women* and *A Feminist Tarot* (with Susan Rennie), both published by Alyson Publications. She has appeared in the documentary films "Word Is Out" and "The Times of Harvey Milk" and is a professor of Speech Communication at San Francisco State University.

Jewelle L. Gomez is the assistant director of the Literature Program of the New York State Council on the Arts. She writes book reviews for "Belle Lettres," "The Village Voice," and "Hurricane Alice." She is currently working on a vampire novel.

Marilyn Krysl has published two books of short stories: *Honey, You've Been Dealt A Winning Hand* (Capra) and *Mozart, Westmoreland and Me* (Thunder's Mouth Press). She has published three volumes of poetry, and her stories and poems have also appeared in magazines. She teaches at the University of Colorado, Boulder.

Jane Lazarre is the author of *The Mother Knot* (Beacon), *On Loving Men* (Dial), *Some Kind of Innocence* (Dial) and *The Powers of Charlotte* (The Crossing Press). Her essays and short stories have appeared in numerous journals and magazines. She teaches writing and women's literature at the Eugene Lang College of the New School for Social Research.

Carolina Mancuso has written for the theater and is an editor in the field of international education. "Mamie" is her first published short story. She is currently working on a novel set in thirteenth century France, told from the viewpoint of an elderly peasant woman.

Harriet Malinowitz has published fiction, articles and reviews, primarily on the subjects of feminism and Central America. She has recently completed her first play, "Minus One." She teaches writing at Hofstra University/District 65's Institute of Applied Social Science, a college program for adult workers. She is presently working on her doctorate at New York University.

Yvonne Pepin has published two books which describe her solitary life in the Oregon mountains: *Cabin Journal* and *Three Summers*, both published by Shameless Hussy Press. She is currently working on a movie script based on these books. She now lives in Port Townsend, Washington, where she and her partner own and operate an art gallery.

Ann Viola is the co-founder of the Adirondack Council for the Disabled, and serves on the Advisory Board of the Center for Independent Living. She is writing a novel that she hopes will help to alter some of the stereotyped ways disabled people have been portrayed in literature.

Sylvia A. Watanabe teaches English in Hayward, California. In 1985 she won the Japanese American Citizens League National Literary Award for her short story, "Colors." Her work has appeared in *The Stories We Hold Secret* (Greenfield Review Press).

Irene Zahava (editor) has been the owner of a feminist bookstore in Ithaca, New York since 1981. She is the editor of *Hear the Silence: Stories of Myth, Magic and Renewal* and *The WomanSleuth Anthology: Contemporary Mystery Stories by Women.*

The Crossing Press Feminist Series includes the following titles:

Abeng, A Novel by Michelle Cliff

All Good Women, A Novel by Valerie Miner

Class Porn, A Novel by Molly Hite

Clenched Fists, Burning Crosses, A Novel by Chris South

Crystal Visions, Nine Meditations for Personal and Planetary Peace by Diane Mariechild

A Faith of One's Own: Explorations by Catholic Lesbians, edited by Barbara Zanotti

Feminist Spirituality and the Feminine Divine, An Annotated Bibliography by Anne Carson

Going Out of Our Minds: The Metaphysics of Liberation, by Sonia Johnson

Hear The Silence: Stories by Women of Myth, Magic and Renewal, edited by Irene Zahava

The Inner Dance: A Guide to Spiritual and Psychological Unfolding by Diane Mariechild

Lesbian Etiquette, Humorous Essays by Gail Sausser

Lesbian Images, Literary Commentary by Jane Rule

Love, Struggle and Change: Stories by Women, edited by Irene Zahava

Magic Mommas, Trembling Sisters, Puritans & Perverts, Feminist Essays by Joanna Russ

Mother, Sister, Daughter, Lover, Stories by Jan Clausen

Mother Wit: A Feminist Guide to Psychic Development by Diane Mariechild

Movement, A Novel by Valerie Miner

Nice Jewish Girls: A Lesbian Anthology, edited by Evelyn Torton Beck

The Politics of Reality: Essays in Feminist Theory by Marilyn Frye

On Strike Against God, A Lesbian Love Story by Joanna Russ

The Queen of Wands, Poetry by Judy Grahn

The Question She Put to Herself, Short Stories by Maureen Brady

Red Beans & Rice, Recipes for Lesbian Health and Wisdom by Bode Noonan

Sinking, Stealing, A Novel by Jan Clausen

Sister Outsider, Essays and Speeches by Audre Lorde

We Are Everywhere, Writings by and About Lesbian Parents, edited by Harriet Alpert

Winter's Edge, A Novel by Valerie Miner

The Work of A Common Woman, Poetry by Judy Grahn

Zami: A New Spelling of My Name, Biomythography by Audre Lorde